Praise for

Soul Ties:

"Shows depth of knowledge in spiritual matters and provides practical prayers and guidance for self deliverance. It's also a good reference to go back to for maintaining spiritual health."

— CARLYN TELFER

"Great read! Scripture is broken down in laymen's terms. Book provides great understanding of soul ties and how to break them! All scripturally based! Must read!"

— SHAMEIKA

"This book unmasks the devil's tactics of using ungodly soul ties to hold a God's child from shining for Jesus. The authors spiritual gift, practical Christian life, powerful prayers, insight to biblical doctrines and experience in deliverance ministry make me prefer this book."

— SUBHASHREE DANIEL

"Thanks for the prayer points. I have heard about soul ties before however I love how this pastor gives you actual prayer points to pray. When you are trying to pray and can't focus because kids are trying to get your attention all kinds of ways, it helps to have the points written down."

— PATRICIA A.

"Love the Book! If you are a Deliverance Minister in this book are some things you'll need to know! Pastor JE Charles used his years of experience in deliverance to equip you with the enemy does not want you to have an in-depth understanding of."

— MRS. CUSTOMER

"In my candid opinion its book you want to have to break free from unhealthy relationships"

— AMAZON CUSTOMER

"Encourage others to buy the book. Very inspiring and good."

— MAMAADEL

Additional works by J.E. Charles
available on Amazon and Dunamis Bookstore

"Divine Encounter: 40-Day Journey to Total Freedom, Healing, and Prosperity"
"Wrestle For Your Destiny: Finding God's Purpose and Power for Your Life"
"Let My People Go!: 21 Days of Fasting And Prayer for Breakthrough and Deliverance"
"Cross Over To Your Inheritance: 7 Days of Prayer Arrows"
"The Power Of 3:00 AM and The Mystery of The Watches"
"Return To Sender: Reversing Witchcraft Curses"
"Crushing the Works of Witchcraft"
"40 Days Fasting and Prayer Guide"
"A Beginner's Guide to Self-Deliverance"
"Healing Your Poisoned Family Tree: Revoking Evil Ancestral Vows"
"Conquer Spiritual Spouses"
"Silence the Voice of the Accuser"
"Sever the Soul Ties"

SOUL TIES

40 DAYS DETOX FROM HARMFUL RELATIONSHIPS AND HEAL YOUR CRUSHED HEART

J.E. CHARLES

A publication of
Dunamis Christian Community | Upper Room Fire Prayer Ministry
P.O Box 12352 Pleasanton CA 94588
Printed in the United States of America

Copyright Permission

Soul Ties: 40-Day Detox from Harmful Relationships to Heal Your Crushed Heart

© 2021 by J.E Charles
A publication of Dunamis Publishing House
| Upper Room Fire Prayer Ministry
P.O. Box 340507, Jamaica, NY 11234
Printed in the United States of America

All rights reserved. No part of this publication may be reproduced, stored in a retrieval system or be transmitted in any form or by any means, mechanical, electronic, photocopying or otherwise without prior written consent of the publisher.

Unless otherwise noted, all Scripture quotations are taken from the New King James Version, copyright © 1979, 1980, 1982 by Thomas Nelson, Inc.

Products are available at special quantity discounts for bulk purchase for sales promotion, premiums, fund-raising, and educational needs.
For details contact us at P. O. Box 12352, Pleasanton, CA 94588 or www.dunamisbookstore.com. Email: sales@upperroomfireprayer.org or Call 408 508 4304
Library of Congress Cataloging in-Publication Data: An application to register this book for cataloging has been submitted to the Library of Congress.

International Standard Book Number:
ISBN: 978-1-7362288-7-6

Pastor J. E. Charles
Dunamis Publishing House
P.O. Box 340507, Jamaica, NY 11234
Email: info@upperroomfireprayer.org
Web: dunamisbookstore.com
Phone: +1 347.208 3605

DISCLAIMER

The information provided in this book is not to be taken for medical or professional advice under any circumstances. By using the information contained in this book, the user assumes full responsibility for his or her actions and agrees that Pastor J. E. Charles will not be held liable or responsible for any consequences that come as a result of the actions taken based on reading the information contained herein.

The reader understands that no promises of success are made to the readers of this book. By reading this book you agree and understand that nothing said herein is meant to give medical, legal, or financial advice and should not be used in place of medical, legal, or financial advice from a qualified expert. If you are in need of legal, financial, or medical help, seek professional help and do not use the information in this book as a substitute for the guidance and advice of certified, qualified experts under any circumstances. Always be sure that you adhere to and obey the government, the laws, and the authorities of your country.

*To the person of the Holy Spirit,
who is the very reason for my being,
and
to my children, Faith and Ike, who should carry this
message of the gospel of Christ to their generation.*

CONTENTS

Preface..xi
Acknowledgements...xiii
Introduction..xv

Day 1	What Are Soul Ties?...1
Day 2	How Soul Ties Are Formed..4
Day 3	Evaluating Ungodly Soul Ties....................................8
Day 4	Exposing Ungodly Soul Ties.....................................11
Day 5	Examining Ungodly Soul Ties..................................15
Day 6	Cords of False Identity..19
Day 7	Deceptive Self-Talk...26
Day 8	Cords of Unforgivingness..31
Day 9	Fountains of Ungodly Soul Ties...............................35
Day 10	Ungodly Relationships..39
Day 11	Ungodly Ties with Believers....................................43
Day 12	Generational Soul Ties..47
Day 13	Freedom from the Curse of the Law........................51
Day 14	The Super Glue of Soul Ties...................................56
Day 15	Digging Deeper Into Relationships.........................61
Day 16	The Cosmic Battle..64
Day 17	Born of a Virgin...68
Day 18	The Death Blow...73
Day 19	Silver Cord Portals..78
Day 20	Accursed Objects..82
Day 21	Blood Covenants..86
Day 22	Unholy Affections...91
Day 23	Soul Ties and Sin..96
Day 24	Demonic Introjection..100
Day 25	Soul Fragmentation..105

Day 26	Soul Wounds	111
Day 27	Sever Ungodly Soul Ties	117
Day 28	The Act of Forgiveness	122
Day 29	Receiving Forgiveness	127
Day 30	Expressions of Godly Soul Ties	133
Day 31	Forming Godly Soul Ties	136
Day 32	Navigating Godly Soul Ties	140
Day 33	Cords of Negative Emotions	144
Day 34	Cords of Anger	148
Day 35	Cords of Fear	153
Day 36	Ungodly Fear	158
Day 37	Cords of Depression	164
Day 38	Cords of Pride	171
Day 39	Cords of Guilt	179
Day 40	Celebrating Freedom	184

About the Author 191

PREFACE

Always be ready to give a defense to everyone who asks you a reason for the hope that is in you, with meekness and fear.
1 Peter 3:15

God, in His infinite wisdom, created every human being with the potential and abilities they need to enjoy fulfilling and godly relationships. Sadly, many people pass through life without ever experiencing the fullness of close, loving relationships as God designed. Others stay captive to toxic relationships, habits, and demonic influences that do not allow them to enjoy the fullness of God's design in human interactions. A select few are able to experience total freedom in relationships, which results in the ability to be who God has designed them to be.

Soul Ties: 40-Day Detox from Harmful Relationships to Heal Your Crushed Heart is a book grounded in the rich teachings of God's Word on relationships and the cords that bind them. Each chapter begins with a devotional aimed at understanding God, relationships, and the ploys Satan uses to hold us in bondage to destructive people and behaviors. Plus, there are questions to help you apply the material to your life and prayers to help you break free from negative people, emotions, habits, and powers. Many chapters also include Bible verses to help you gain total victory in all your relationships.

The Dunamis Christian Center | Upper Room Fire Prayer Ministry is a center for freedom and prayer, with a vision to transforming lives globally. connecting people to Jesus Christ through discipleship, while equipping everyone with the life-changing principles of abundant life.

Our principal focus is praying, and we are passionate about praying for others. We believe that we should *"Make the most of every opportunity"* (Ephesians 5:16, NLT) as the Bible instructs. The inspired Word of our God is the tool that prepares our hands for war and our fingers for battle! (Psalm 144:1). When we study God's Word, apply the principles, and pray for God's power, we can see the fullness of the relationships that God has for us. Total freedom from toxic relationships comes by severing ungodly soul ties, cutting the cords that bind, and creating godly relationships that bring life to the soul and healing to the body.

Engage the material with firm determination and holy vigor. Answer the questions. Pray the prayers. Meditate upon the Scriptures. Your relationships will never be the same.

We pray that the hand of God will become more visible in your relationships as you meditate upon this material and call out to God in faith.

Yours on the Altar of Prayer,
Pastor Charles and Lady Akuss

ACKNOWLEDGEMENTS

Do not withhold good from those to whom it is due,
When it is in the power of your hand to do so.
Proverbs 3:27

I hereby acknowledge all the people who were used by Almighty God in times past to guide me and others for the coming of our Lord Jesus Christ.

I acknowledge Dr. D. K. Olukoya, a man sent by God, who faithfully proclaims the Word of God and understands the power of persistent prayer. His ministry has touched me and blessed my family in innumerable ways. His methods of spreading the Word have transformed this generation's prayer methodology. I extend thanks to everyone at the Freedom and Deliverance Ministry of the Well Christian Community Church. My sincere hope is that the Lord blesses and keeps them until He comes again.

Thank you, Mischelle Sandowich, for your many helpful suggestions and contributions as an editor.

Finally, I express thanks, love, and dedication to Lady Akuss, my wife, for her unwavering support. She not only supports me and this ministry, but also fulfills the practical roles of editor and art advisor.

INTRODUCTION

The righteous should choose his friends carefully, For the way of the wicked leads them astray.

Proverbs 12:26

Are you prepared to embark on a life-changing journey in your relationships through the power of God? Before you begin, we want to give you a taste of what to expect in *Soul Ties: 40-Day Detox from Harmful Relationships to Heal Your Crushed Heart*.

What to Expect

What do you desire to see in your relationships? We're not talking about just romantic relationships, but even those close connections with friends and family. Below is a list of common desires among men and women in all kinds of relationships. Do you:

- Desire to be loved and respected?
- Wish to be treated with kindness?
- Want your friends to really listen to you?
- Yearn to know that someone genuinely cares for you?
- Want friends that won't talk behind your back?
- Who are trustworthy to a fault?
- Who give as much as they take (or more)?
- And just like to hang out?
- They love you just the way you are!
- Are not afraid to tell the truth!
- Speak well of you and others!
- And genuinely care about other people.

Are these things important to you? Would you like to have this in all of your relationships?

We all desire to have close relationships with trusted friends and spouses. But sometimes, no matter how hard we try to make our relationships work, they just fall apart at the seams. Often, we get trapped in abusive situations and all we get is hurt and pain. Soon, we might start repeating the lies of the enemy: I'll never have a good relationship; No one will ever want to marry me; Everyone wants to hurt me.

If that's you, we have some GREAT news. God can heal your broken relationships and help you thrive in friendships, family, and marriage. All the secrets to healthy relationships are in the Bible. And they begin by severing ungodly soul ties and embracing godly relationships as God designed. All these secrets to total success and freedom in your relationships are revealed in *Soul Ties: 40-Day Detox from Harmful Relationships to Heal Your Crushed Heart*.

One thing is true, healing from broken relationships is not always easy; but it is always good. If you do the hard work, read the chapters, answer the questions, pray the prayers, and meditate upon God's Holy Word, you will start to experience relationships the way God designed.

How to Prepare

Preparing for your journey will prime your heart and mind for the work ahead. Let's look at seven things that will give you the best chance of success over the next 40 days.

1. **Faith:** The primary factor of whether you will have success on your journey is your level of faith. *"But without faith it is impossible to please Him, for he who comes to God must believe that He is, and that He is a rewarder of those who diligently seek Him"* (Hebrews 11:6). Do you believe in the promises of God for your good? Do you believe that He will reward you if you diligently seek Him? Pray daily for the faith to believe the Word of God as you work through this manual for relationship healing.
2. **Diligence:** *"The lazy man does not roast what he took in hunting, But diligence is a man's precious possession"* (Proverbs 12:27). If you want to get the most out of *Soul Ties*, you cannot apply yourself half-heartedly. You must read every page, paragraph, and word. Answer every question with honesty and humility. Pray the prayers, and believe the Scriptures. Give every advantage to your soul. Do not be like the lazy man who doesn't even eat the food he catches.
3. **Commitment:** Before you start this journey, commit to seeing it through to the end. There may be chapters that hurt really bad. Sometimes we have to hurt before we can heal. Don't start Chapter One until you commit to spending 40 solid days with the book. Mark it on

your calendar. Tell your friends. Find an accountability partner. Whatever it takes, commit to seeing the book through to the end.

4. **Understanding:** God is the one who grants understanding, wisdom, and knowledge. As you work through this book, ask Him to enlighten your eyes that you may understand what He is trying to teach you each day. Ask for the illumination of the Holy Spirit.

5. **Salvation:** If you do not know the Lord Jesus Christ as your Savior, commit your life to Him today. Healing apart from Christ is temporary at best. Repent of your sins and ask Him to be the Lord of your life today. Eternity is at stake.

6. **Humility:** "*Yes, all of you be submissive to one another, and be clothed with humility, for 'God resists the proud, But gives grace to the humble'*" (1 Peter 5:5). Humility is a work in progress with us all. You need God's grace to make it through this journey. God resists the proud. If you hold on to a proud heart, God will not be able to heal your relationships.

7. **Action:** The final step to prepare is to be prepared to take action. Throughout this journey, you will be challenged to sever the harmful cords in your life. You must be prepared to take the necessary steps. If you take no action, God will not heal your relationships. "*But do you want to know, O foolish man, that faith without works is dead?*" (James 2:20). Ask God to prepare you to be a doer of the Word and not merely a hearer. "*But be doers of the word, and not hearers only, deceiving yourselves*" (James 1:22).

Well, beloved, there is only one thing left to do. That is to start on "Day One" of your *40-Day Detox from Harmful Relationships to Heal Your Crushed Heart.* May God richly bless you with marvelous healing in all your relationships as you embark on your journey. Amen!

DAY ONE

WHAT ARE SOUL TIES?

The soul of Jonathan was knit to the soul of David,
and Jonathan loved him as his own soul.
1 SAMUEL 18:1

Proverbs speaks of a friend that sticks closer than a brother. Perhaps you've had (or have) a friend that you love so dearly that they feel like family to you.

While the phrase "soul ties" does not appear in Scripture, the idea can be found in many places. I will share some specific examples from the Bible shortly. But first, let's get a working definition.

The soul is not located in a specific part of the body. Nor does it exist separate from the body. Rather, a soul comprises the entire person, representing the body's life force (spirit) as joined to the body. "*And the Lord God formed man of the dust of the ground, and breathed into his nostrils the breath of life; and man became a living being* [soul]" (Genesis 2:7).

A "soul tie" refers to a close, knitting-together or special bonding between two (or more) souls.

Soul Ties in the Bible

Below are three examples of relationships in the Bible where the bond was so intimate, it could be described as a soul tie:

- **David and Jonathan:** These two friends' souls were "*knit*" together in godly love (1 Samuel 18:1). They sacrificed and cared for one another in a special way.
- **Paul and Onesimus:** Paul was Onesimus' spiritual father, and he loved him as his "*own heart*" (Philemon 1:12).
- **Jacob and Benjamin:** Jacob was grieved of his beloved son Joseph. As a result, Jacob's heart was especially tied to Benjamin, causing his life to be "*bound up in the lad's life*" (Genesis 44:30).

These passages show that close relationships can (and often do) form soul ties. These ties can be among friends, family members, spiritual leaders, and more. Soul ties also exist in marriage (Genesis 2:24) and in our relationship with the Lord (1 Samuel 13:14).

The examples listed above are good and natural. In fact, God has created soul ties for many good purposes:

1. God desires His children to have close relationships and spiritual fellowship with one another.
2. Godly soul ties attract a husband and wife together romantically and help them grow together as they live out their days.
3. A spiritual connection helps children bond with their parents and parents with their children.
4. God wants to connect to His children in a special way.

However, in everything good that God does, Satan seeks to counterfeit. Therefore, we must be aware of forming ungodly soul ties.

Ungodly Soul Ties

The same word that describes how Jonathan and David's souls were "knit" together can have a very negative connotation, even "conspiring" together for evil purposes. We must avoid ungodly alliances if we seek to live the abundant life that Jesus has designed for us.

The Bible warns, *"My son, if sinners entice you, do not consent"* and *"do not go along with them"* (Proverbs 1:10,15). We should not join forces with wicked men to do sinful things.

I Corinthians 6:16 warns of another kind of ungodly soul tie: *"Or do you not know that he who is joined to a harlot is one body with her? For 'the two,' He says, 'shall become one flesh.'"*

In the next chapter, we will discuss how godly and ungodly soul ties form.

Wrapping Up

If you have never studied the theology of soul ties, please do not be overwhelmed. This first chapter merely touches the surface of the topic. All these themes and ideas will be expanded upon in future chapters. You are embarking on a life-changing journey to abundant, healthy relationships — and godly soul ties.

Now, it is time to do a little homework to help digest this material and begin to apply it to your life. Enjoy this process. God has good things planned for you over the next 40 days — if you do your part.

HOMEWORK

1. Evaluate your life, and list any godly or ungodly relationships that you might have in your life. Use additional paper if you need more room.

Godly Relationships	Ungodly Relationships

2. Ask God to search your heart to reveal any and all ungodly soul ties in your life.

DAY TWO

HOW SOUL TIES ARE FORMED

*So then, they are no longer two but one flesh. Therefore what
God has joined together, let not man separate.*
MATTHEW 19:6

God has established laws in the universe that guide how all things operate. For example, we learn in chemistry that negatively charged particles are attracted to positively charged particles. Due to this "attraction," atoms are formed. These atoms then become the building blocks for all matter.

Something similar happens in relationships. There is an unseen force that pulls us in and "ties" us together in a special bond, friendship, or partnership. This is part of God's design for the human race to propagate and flourish. When we see an interesting or attractive person, something outside of our control (or so it seems), draws us to them. If pursued, the relationship can lead to marriage or a life-long friendship.

Parents, children, and other family members experience a similar draw. A mother bonds with her new baby. A brother learns to cherish his baby sister. We grow close to aunts, uncles, and cousins because they are specially connected to us.

These relationships are designed by God. He has created something special inside of our souls that causes us to stick together with those godly, natural relationships. God is the author of all godly soul ties.

Broken People and Relationships

However, because of the fall (when Adam sinned and God cursed the earth), relationships don't always work the way God designed. Sometimes a mother doesn't love her child the way she ought. Or a father abuses his son or daughter physically, verbally, or sexually. Maybe another family member hurts us. Or perhaps a friend (or someone dear) betrays us or lies to us.

These negative emotional experiences create a void in our hearts that can attract us to the wrong kind of person, behavior, or relationship. Often, people don't even know why they make bad choices, seek out the wrong kind of relationships, and engage in behaviors that are harmful to themselves. Sometimes the results are so severe, they lead to deep soul wounds and even soul fragmentation. We will talk more about these in future chapters.

Natural Reactions to Brokenness

It is common and natural to respond to these difficulties by making sinful or harmful choices. Perhaps a person will use drugs, alcohol, or sexual promiscuity to escape the pain. An abused person might be attracted to a controlling and violent person. Often, this happens without even knowing why. It just feels natural. And in our fallen state, it is natural.

However, sin and the perpetuation of abuse are never good. These natural responses are bad choices that only bring further harm. And they can introduce damaging connections to darkness through the spirit world, leading people into deeper hardships and addictions.

So why does this happen?

Ungodly Soul Ties Are Formed

Satan always seeks to kill, steal, and destroy. And he loves to counterfeit the things of God. Satan knows how to operate within God's rules of attraction to create "counterfeit" soul ties — or ungodly soul ties.

There are two primary ways Satan works to form ungodly soul ties: through inheritance and sin.

Inheritance: The human race has inherited the sin of Adam. Plus, God has ordained that the sins of our parents are passed on to the children to the third and fourth generation (Exodus 20:5). If we have an abusive or sinful parent, we will inherit their sins and suffer the repercussions in our life unless God intervenes. Our ancestral line can open our lives up to the same demonic activity that plagued our parents.

Sin: We don't merely inherit sin from our ancestors, we also willfully choose to sin (it seems natural). When we "decide" to sin, we open ourselves up to additional demonic influences that can lock us up into deeper sinful behavior. We create our own "soul ties" with people that God never intended for us and grant demons permission to bring destruction into our lives.

In future chapters, we will delve deeper into these unholy bonds which are powered by hell instead of heaven. But for now, let's take a quick look at some specific ways we can create both godly and ungodly soul ties.

Biblical Survey of Soul Ties

Below are some common ways to enter into soul ties as expressed in the Bible.

- **Marriage:** "*For this reason a man shall leave his father and mother and be joined to his wife, and the two shall become one flesh*" (Ephesians 5:31).
- **Sexual Immorality:** "*Or do you not know that he who is joined to a harlot is one body with her? For 'the two,' He says, 'shall become one flesh'*" (1 Corinthians 6:16).
- **Friendship:** "*Now when he had finished speaking to Saul, the soul of Jonathan was knit to the soul of David, and Jonathan loved him as his own soul*" (I Samuel 18:1).
- **Sinful Alliances:** "*My son, if sinners entice you, Do not consent. If they say, 'Come with us, Let us lie in wait to shed blood; Let us lurk secretly for the innocent without cause'*" (Proverbs 1:10-11).
- **Family:** "*Now therefore, when I come to your servant my father, and the lad is not with us, since his life is bound up in the lad's life*" (Genesis 44:30).
- **Inheritance:** "*And the Lord passed before him and proclaimed, "The Lord, the Lord God, merciful and gracious, longsuffering, and abounding in goodness and truth, keeping mercy for thousands, forgiving iniquity and transgression and sin, by no means clearing the guilty, visiting the iniquity of the fathers upon the children and the children's children to the third and the fourth generation*" (Exodus 34:6-8).
- **Spiritual Children:** "*I appeal to you for my son Onesimus, whom I have begotten while in my chains, who once was unprofitable to you, but now is profitable to you and to me. I am sending him back. You therefore receive him, that is, my own heart*" (Philemon 1:10-12).
- **Vows and Covenants:** "*If a man makes a vow to the Lord, or swears an oath to bind himself by some agreement, he shall not break his word; he shall do according to all that proceeds out of his mouth*" (Numbers 30:2).
- **Deep Affections:** "*But the poor man had nothing, except one little ewe lamb which he had bought and nourished; and it grew up together with him and with his children. It ate of his own food and drank from his own cup and lay in his bosom; and it was like a daughter to him*" (2 Samuel 12:3).
- **Unholy Affections:** "*Ephraim is joined to idols, Let him alone. Their drink is rebellion, They commit harlotry continually. Her rulers dearly love dishonor* (Hosea 4:17).

Now that we have examined some Scriptural reasons for soul ties, let's examine our own hearts by answering the following questions.

HOMEWORK

Answer the following questions:

1. Who creates godly soul ties? List several examples of godly soul ties.

2. How can Satan take a good soul tie and turn it into something evil?

3. Look at the "Biblical Survey of Soul Ties" above and identify which soul ties are godly.

4. Can you identify any ungodly soul ties in your life? Write them down here.

Prayer: Father, help me identify any ungodly soul ties in my life and strengthen the godly soul ties that I have.

DAY THREE

EVALUATING UNGODLY SOUL TIES

Do not be unequally yoked together with unbelievers. For what fellowship has righteousness with lawlessness? And what communion has light with darkness?
2 Corinthians 6:14

To plow a field, farmers need to trench the earth in straight lines. By yoking two oxen together, they can work more efficiently, increasing the "horse" power — or in this case, the "ox" power. However, if the oxen are not equal in strength or size, the results can be disastrous. The oxen may run in circles or may not even be able to accomplish the assigned task. The farmer would be better off working with a single ox, or even alone.

The same thing happens in the lives of Christians. When we are yoked together with someone or something that is not a right fit for us spiritually, we can experience the devastations of unequal yoking or ungodly soul ties. All our efforts at successful, joyful Christian living can be thwarted. Our lives may seem to be only running around in circles. Just like the farmer, we can operate much better (and be more productive in life) by casting off these ungodly yokes and ties.

And there is good news! Because Jesus Christ sacrificed His life on the cross, we are promised triumph over these ungodly bonds. "*Stand fast therefore in the liberty by which Christ has made us free, and do not be entangled again with a yoke of bondage*" (Galatians 5:1).

Symptoms of Ungodly Soul Ties

Since we are often blinded to the things that harm us, it can be difficult to identify ungodly soul ties. One way to help break through the haze is to evaluate our physical, spiritual, and mental condition. This can help us recognize the existence of ungodly soul ties so we can get to the root cause. Below is a list of symptoms that can result from ungodly soul ties in your life. See if you recognize any of these symptoms in your life.

1. Depression
2. Anxiety
3. Panic
4. Grief
5. Fear
6. Addictions
7. Thoughts of Suicide
8. Mental Illness
9. Heart Disease
10. Cancer
11. Arthritis
12. Demonic Manifestations
13. Difficulty Forming Godly Relationships
14. Jealousy
15. Bad Dreams

This list is not exhaustive. There may be additional manifestations of ungodly soul ties in your life. If any area of your life is not operating according to God's perfect peace, it could be an indicator of an ungodly soul tie. On the flip side, just because you have one or more of these symptoms does not mean that you necessarily have an ungodly soul tie. There may be other reasons for these issues in your life. However, they should be warning signals that cause you to evaluate. Perhaps the root is an ungodly soul tie.

Hope for Ungodly Soul Ties

As mentioned previously, soul ties can emerge from inheritance or by actual sins like unequally yoked relationships, premarital sexual experiences, and vows and contracts that violate God's laws. We create these unhealthy soul ties and thus become imbued with the same sin and negativity of the person the bond connects us to.

It is important to pray through and evaluate these common sources of ungodly soul ties so you can begin to take dominion of the source and weed out the root causes. We will be doing more examination in the following days.

Ultimately, Jesus Christ and His work on the cross holds the power over all these things. Ungodly bonds that humans cannot break on their own can be destroyed with God's authority. When a person repents of their sin and accepts Christ as Lord and Savior, then God adopts them into His family. Now, they can claim His inheritance and His authority in their lives. Satan no longer holds dominion over them. But each person must renounce their sins, the sins of their ancestors, and their ungodly relationships.

HOMEWORK

Answer the following questions:

1. Are there any relationships in your life that you think do not please God? List them.

2. In what ways can being unequally yoked bring harm into your life?

3. Do you suffer from any of the "symptoms" of ungodly soul ties? List each one.

4. How can you break the bonds of ungodly soul ties?

5. Have you repented of your sins and asked Jesus to be your Lord and Savior?

Prayer: Father, forgive me of my sins. Reveal any ungodly soul ties in my life. Grant me the power to break them, in Jesus' name.

DAY FOUR

EXPOSING UNGODLY SOUL TIES

*And have no fellowship with the unfruitful works
of darkness, but rather expose them.*
EPHESIANS 5:11

When a computer slows down, stops working, or gets a virus, we can't fix the problem until we know what is causing it. We must run diagnostic tests to identify the root cause of the problem. And that's what we are going to do today. As a reminder, yesterday, we looked at some symptoms of ungodly soul ties. Today, we are going to run some diagnostics to examine what the root causes of these symptoms might be.

Self-Examination

Let's evaluate if any of the bonds you have formed in your life are ungodly. Below is a series of questions to help you diagnose if you have any ungodly soul ties.

1. **Have you willingly yoked yourself in a relationship that doesn't honor God?** An unequally yoked relationship could include marriage to or dating an unbeliever, a business relationship with an ungodly partner, a pact with someone to bring harm upon another, taking a job that requires you to break the commands of God, a close friendship with an unbeliever, or any other relationship that brings dishonor to God. Do everything you can lawfully to unhitch relationships that dishonors God. There are exceptions in marriage between a man and a woman (see 1 Corinthians 7:12-16).

2. **Have you taken any vows, made any covenants, or entered into any agreements that break God's commandments?** Have you entered into a "marriage" union with someone

of the same sex? God does not honor this. You must separate from this godless union and renounce all soul ties. Have you promised your heart to someone hastily and then walked away from the relationship? Renounce that soul tie. Have you shaken hands with someone in agreement for something that does not honor God? Have you agreed to take on debt that you cannot afford? Are you signing paperwork that you do not understand? Always be extremely careful before you agree to anything. Renounce all ungodly contracts spiritually and legally.

3. **Have you or are you engaging in sexual relationships outside of marriage?** God says the marriage bed is to remain undefiled. Sexual relationships of all kinds are only permitted in a marriage between a man and a woman, preferably with a godly man and godly woman. Any foreplay, inappropriate touching, passionate kissing, intercourse, masturbation, and other sexual promiscuity outside of marriage is forbidden. Plus, pornography, bestiality, homosexuality, and other perverted practices are strictly forbidden in or out of marriage. All these acts create ungodly soul ties that can cause much destruction in your life and the lives of your loved ones. Renounce these through the power of Jesus Christ.

4. **Are you allowing someone to control you?** This includes any friend, acquaintance, family member, employee, employer, leader in your church, member in your church, or neighbor. If anyone is "forcing" or "coercing" you to do something that you do not want to do, believe is wrong, or is not lawful — and you allow them to influence your behavior negatively, you need to break free. Repent and take steps to remove yourself from this person's control in the power of the Holy Spirit. Jesus says, *"But let your 'Yes' be 'Yes,' and your 'No,' 'No.' For whatever is more than these is from the evil one"* (Matthew 5:37).

5. **Are you overly interested in someone or something that does not lawfully belong to you?** Unholy affections create unholy soul ties that can devastate your life. You are opening yourself up to demonic activity that can destroy you and those you love. Perhaps you are "obsessed" with a woman or man who is married to another. Maybe you are "enamored" by a movie star or celebrity. Have your affections toward a favorite pastor or teacher enticed you to sit at the front of the church service, desire to be close to them, or follow unreasonable urges to connect with them? Repent. Or perhaps you "cherish" the inappropriate advances or glances from the opposite sex. These kinds of ungodly bonds, if not surrendered at the feet of Jesus, can grant permission to demons to bring evil and mayhem into your life.

6. **Do you covet stuff that belongs to someone else?** We are commanded in Scripture not to covet stuff that belongs to other people, including success, spouses, wealth, belongings,

or anything else that belongs to another. When we desire these things, we can open up a doorway for a demon to cling to us and torment us. Confess your ungodly desires and forsake them. Ask God to remove any ungodly soul ties that may have formed as a result.

7. **Are your pets more important than people?** There is nothing sinful about loving your domesticated animals. However, some people love their animals more than they love people, who are created in the image of God. Also, our affection for our animals must be subject to the law of God (as must all things). For example, God forbids bestiality. If you have sexual desires for your animals or engage in this type of behavior, you must repent quickly, as this type of soul tie is an abomination to the Lord. The Lord Jesus can deliver you.

8. **Have you gladly received an ungodly gift?** Pastor Phillip Kayser tells the story of how his wife received an "idol" as a gift from a Korean student who came to live with them. Immediately, she fell ill. The sickness left after they discarded the gift and asked God to remove the demonic influence.[1] Some wicked people will bestow cursed gifts upon others, establishing a bond that allows the demonic forces to work their evil ways on the victim. Do not accept gifts from people you do not know, nor from people that you know are involved in occult practices or witchcraft. If you do not know the person well enough — or you know the gift is demonic — reject the gift. Also, inspect your home for objects of evil (pornographic images, telephone numbers or websites of prostitutes and drug suppliers, idols, magic books, games, and cards, objects used in occult practices, etc.).

Each of the above scenarios can grant people and demons the power to manipulate and damage you, affect your dreams, and torment you. People touched by evil and hatred welcome and/or use these negative soul ties to inflict pain on unprotected people. These people are working in accordance with Satan. Reject them. *"The thief does not come except to steal, and to kill, and to destroy"* (John 10:10).

Separating from these schemes and behaviors is the only way to deal with these ungodly soul ties a death blow. And it can only be done in the power of Jesus Christ. You must always be extremely cautious when entering new relationships and take special care to evaluate existing ones.

---

[1] "Do Demons Know Your Name?" https://kaysercommentary.com/Sermons/New%20Testament/Acts/Acts%2019/Acts%2019_11-16.md (Accessed 3/5/21)

HOMEWORK

Prayerfully read through the list of eight questions above. Honestly evaluate your life in all eight areas. On a separate piece of paper or in a prayer journal, write down a statement for each area, evaluating any potential ungodly soul ties in your life. We've included an example to follow below. Answer the questions truthfully between you and God. Then, ask God to help you break these ties.

1. **Have you willingly yoked yourself in a relationship that doesn't honor God?**

    Example: I am not married to an unbeliever, but I am dating someone who I know is not a Christian. Plus, my best friend is a Buddhist and is always asking me to pray with them.

    Example Prayer: Father, help me break these soul ties in the power of Your Spirit. You have commanded me not to be yoked together with an unbeliever. Help me share the gospel of Jesus Christ with my friend.

Prayer: Father, grant me the power and wisdom to honestly evaluate my life for ungodly soul ties and give me the power to break them in Jesus' name.

DAY FIVE

EXAMINING UNGODLY SOUL TIES

*The words of his mouth were smoother than butter, But war
was in his heart; His words were softer than oil,
Yet they were drawn swords.*

PSALM 55:21

In the book of Judges, we read the account of Samson and Delilah. This classic story reveals how ungodly soul ties lead to death and destruction. Samson and Delilah were involved in illicit sexual endeavors. Unbeknownst to Samson, Delilah had conspired to kill him. After several attempts on his life, Samson was too blind to see that he was in danger. Delilah used manipulation to trick Samson to reveal the source of his strength, saying, *"How can you say, 'I love you,' when your heart is not with me?"* (Judges 16:15).

Samson finally gave in to Delilah's control because of her persistence, and she *"lulled him to sleep on her knees"* and had his head shaved to take away his power and strength (Judges 16:19).

Delilah's conspirators overpowered Samson, put out his eyes, made him their slave, and mocked him. He eventually died. Samson's sexual sin blinded his eyes to the obvious plans by Delilah to take away his power and strength. Her actions should have revealed her wicked plans. But Samson was too blinded by raw lust and sweet words to see the wickedness in Delilah's heart.

Actions speak louder than words, and ungodly soul ties blind us to things that can harm us.

Danger Signs in Relationships

In your relationships, you must focus on a person's actions not just their honeyed words. Always remember what real love looks like: *"Love suffers long* [is patient] *and is kind; love does not envy;*

love does not parade itself [by saying look at how good I am], *is not puffed up* [proud]; *does not behave rudely, does not seek its own, is not provoked* [easily angered], *thinks no evil* [doesn't easily accuse you of wrong]; *does not rejoice in iniquity, but rejoices in the truth; bears all things, believes all things, hopes all things, endures all things. Love never fails"* (1 Corinthians 13:4-8).

Consider this list of warning signs that a relationship in your life may be unfruitful, unloving, and not God's best for you.

1. Does this person insist on control and only want to do things their way, or will they be lenient and compromise?
2. Are they egotistical and selfish?
3. Does this person take from others all the time, or do they have a giving spirit?
4. Do they act with love, kindness, and compassion?
5. Are their behaviors manipulative and focused primarily on how you behave?
6. Have they been saved, and do they accept Jesus in their life?

Any bond that includes selfishness, manipulation, or evil motives exists as an ungodly soul tie — and it leaves the weaker person in the relationship open to abuse and control. These soul ties create a connection that puts one person at an unhealthy advantage over the other.

Mental and emotional bondages such as described above are difficult to break from. The person in control can say and do what they want, including forcing the controlled person to act, speak, and think in ways that harm themselves or others. Remember how Delilah used manipulation to get Samson to give away the secret to his strength? It ultimately resulted in his death.

Break Free from Ungodly Soul Ties

When you get stuck in an unhealthy relationship and suffer from relationship-based attacks, you need to destroy the negative soul ties with these people. If someone uses foul language, curses you, rejects God, bears false witness, or seeks to hurt you physically, mentally, or emotionally, you must break free in the power of the Spirit of God.

If you refuse to break the tie, you will be responsible for the negative results. You are allowing the abuse and permitting Satan (and the person) to harm you. And as long as you choose to stay connected to that relationship, the negative situation will continue.

While godly soul ties are akin to strong vines that bear good fruit, ungodly ones are like vines that wrap around you and strangle your life. Plus, these ungodly ties allow evil spirits to cause fear, stress, disorder, illness, and even death. In these cases, you no longer have dominion over your own thoughts and actions.

When one person in a relationship gains control over another, manipulates them, and controls how they think and feel, it is a destructive relationship. These kinds of sinful bonds have an overwhelming effect on the mind, emotions, body, and soul. They must (and can) be broken by the resurrection power of Jesus Christ.

We will continue examining soul ties so that we can have total freedom from all ungodly relationships. Today, for your homework, you will take the "Love Test" to see how your relationships measure up to God's definition of love. Tomorrow, we will start looking at a few of the cords that can hold us in bondage to the wrong people.

HOMEWORK

Love is the foundation of all godly soul ties and should set the standard for all your relationships. God defines love in 1 Corinthians 13:4-8. Make a list of all your relationships and put them to the love test. See how they measure up.

The Love Test

1. Is _____ **patient** with me? (**Y**/N)
2. Is _____ **kind** to me me? (**Y**/N)
3. Does _____ **trust** me and give me the **freedom** to do the things I enjoy? (**Y**/N)
4. Does _____ **boast** about all his/her qualities? (Y/**N**)
5. Does _____ **encourage** me with kind words? (**Y**/N)
6. Is _____ **arrogant** and **puffed up**? (Y/**N**)
7. Is _____ **rude** to me and others? (Y/**N**)
8. Does _____ **consider my needs** and concerns about his/her own? (**Y**/N)
9. Does _____ get **angry** at me for little things? (Y/**N**)
10. Do I always have to **walk on eggshells** around _____? (Y/**N**)
11. Is _____ involved in sinful or **wicked** behavior? (Y/**N**)
12. Does _____ **love truth**? (**Y**/N)
13. Does _____ **accept me** when I make mistakes? (**Y**/N)
14. Does _____ always **question my motives**? (Y/**N**)
15. Does _____ try **see the positive** in me and others? (**Y**/N)
16. Does _____ **threaten** to harm me or stop caring for me? (Y/**N**)

The loving, proper response to each question is in bold (either **Y** or **N**). If your friend, acquaintance, or spouse is demonstrating love toward you, then your answer should correspond to the bold **Y** or **N**. If you have not circled the bold letter, then your friend does not love you as God designed.

Now, test yourself. How do you love your neighbor, friend, or spouse? Change each question accordingly. For example, in question one, ask yourself, "Am I patient with _____?"

DAY SIX

CORDS OF FALSE IDENTITY

Therefore you are no longer a slave but a son, and if a son, then an heir of God through Christ.
GALATIANS 4:7

In the heat of the noon sun, a lone Samaritan woman traveled a long distance to draw water out of a well. The Jews despised her because she was a woman and a Samaritan. Her own people rejected her because she had already been divorced four times and the man she was living with was not her husband. She was an outcast, rejected by all. Yet, Jesus went out of His way to meet with this woman and do the unthinkable: drink water from her cup.

Despite all the ungodly soul ties, soul wounds, and possible fragmentations, this Samaritan woman drank living water that day that would heal her soul. She looked to Jesus and received a new identity: a child of God. She became a great evangelist, leading many souls to Christ. She could have taken another path: wallowed in her sin, rejected her savior, and accepted her identity as unloved and forsaken. Instead, she believed the testimony of Christ.

Have you accepted Christ's testimony about you? Today, we are going on a journey to identify and cast off several cords of false identity that can hold you in bondage to the lies of Satan and unhealthy relationships.

1. Rejected or Accepted?

God never lies. We cannot refuse His testimony about us: in Christ, we are accepted. *"For 'whoever calls on the name of the LORD shall be saved'"* (Romans 10:13) and *"He made us accepted in the Beloved"* (Ephesians 1:6). Yet, some people still struggle to accept themselves, valuing themselves less than God values them.

Self-rejection can occur simply because you do not like yourself at a particular time in your life. You may not think you are good enough to obtain God's favor, or you are ashamed of your sin. Perhaps you feel you have nothing to offer God or others. These ideas are lies from Satan and must be cast off. Are you better than God? He has accepted you. You must also accept yourself. Until you accept God's view of you, it will be impossible for you to have a healthy relationship. Below are some Bible verses to meditate upon if you are rejecting God's testimony about yourself.

1. **Psalm 139:14:** *"I will praise You, for I am fearfully and wonderfully made; Marvelous are Your works, And that my soul knows very well."*
2. **Genesis 1:27:** *"So God created man in His own image; in the image of God He created him; male and female He created them."*

Accept that you are created in the image of God and fearfully and wonderfully made. If God accepts you in Christ, you should also accept who He made you to be.

2. Unloved or Beloved?

If you have experienced a string of rejections or have been abandoned by a caregiver or parent, you may carry a destructive cord of false identity: the belief that you are unloved. Believing that you are not loved is another lie from the pit of hell. The Bible says you are beloved of God. There is nothing that can separate you from that love. However, you must believe what God says about you. Reject the devil's false testimony, and accept the Word of the Living God.

1. **1 John 3:1** *"Behold what manner of love the Father has bestowed on us, that we should be called children of God!"*
2. **Romans 8:38-39:** *"For I am persuaded that neither death nor life, nor angels nor principalities nor powers, nor things present nor things to come, nor height nor depth, nor any other created thing, shall be able to separate us from the love of God which is in Christ Jesus our Lord."*

God loves you. He says nothing can separate you from that love. Since it is true, you might as well believe it and enjoy it.

3. Unworthy or Worthy?

If you have made many mistakes in your life, like the Samaritan woman, you may feel that you are unworthy of love, friendship, blessing, or other good gifts from God. However, our worth does not come from the things we do. Rather, our worth comes from what Christ has done for us. Have you trusted Christ as your Lord and Savior? Then, you are worthy of eternal life and all the spiritual blessings of Christ.

Reject the enemy's attempt to hold you in bondage to the false cord of unworthiness. It is true, in yourself, you are unworthy. In Christ, however, you have all things. If you struggle with worthiness, memorize these verses:

1. **Ephesians 1:3:** *"Blessed be the God and Father of our Lord Jesus Christ, who has blessed us with every spiritual blessing in the heavenly places in Christ."*
2. **2 Corinthians 5:17:** *"Therefore, if anyone is in Christ, he is a new creation; old things have passed away; behold, all things have become new."*

Accept that you are a new creation in Christ with access to every spiritual blessing in the heavenly places. If you are abiding in Christ, you are worthy to walk in white (Revelation 3:4).

4. Mentally Unstable or Whole?

When others have abused you, the tendency is to feel broken, fragmented, and unstable. In Christ, however, you are whole. This is your true identity. It might take some time to recover from the wounds that cause mental uncertainty. However, in Christ, your true identity is whole and healthy with a sound mind.

Cut the cords of Satan's scheme to make you believe your mind is messed up. Reclaim what belongs to you. Be transformed by renewing your mind. That is your right in Christ Jesus. Here are some verses to correct wrong thinking in this area:

1. **2 Timothy 1:7:** *"For God has not given us a spirit of fear, but of power and of love and of a sound mind."*
2. **Romans 12:2:** *"And do not be conformed to this world, but be transformed by the renewing of your mind, that you may prove what is that good and acceptable and perfect will of God."*

God has given you a sound mind. Do you believe it? If not, then be transformed by renewing your mind. Study, meditate upon, and trust God's Word to renew your mind. His Word is true, reliable, and transformational.

5. Fearful or Bold?

When a dog barks, we ought to be afraid. God has given fear as a protective device. Irrational fear, however, comes from the enemy of your soul. What holds you in bondage to fear? If you ever feel afraid to obey God, that is an irrational fear. You should have the boldness to obey God, speak the truth in love, share the gospel with your neighbor, and carry out your normal daily activities. Irrational fears can hold you in bondage. They are not from God.

The Lord has not given you a spirit of fear. Rather, he has granted you boldness. If you are held captive by false cords of fear, cry out to God for deliverance. God is with you. Here are two verses to help deliver you from fear:

1. **Joshua 1:9:** *"Have I not commanded you? Be strong and of good courage; do not be afraid, nor be dismayed, for the Lord your God is with you wherever you go."*
2. **Romans 8:15:** *"For you did not receive the spirit of bondage again to fear, but you received the Spirit of adoption by whom we cry out, 'Abba, Father.'"*

Reject the spirit of fear and accept the boldness that comes through the power of the Holy Spirit. *"And when they had prayed, the place where they were assembled together was shaken; and they were all filled with the Holy Spirit, and they spoke the word of God with boldness* (Acts 4:31).

6. Worthless or Useful?

Feeling worthless is different from feeling unworthy. If you feel worthless, you may believe that God has no plan for your life. This again is a lie from the devil. Satan would like nothing more than to hold you captive to uselessness. Yet, God says He has a plan for your life. You were created for a purpose.

If you ever struggle to know what your purpose is, you can do three things: 1) Be thankful; 2) Rejoice; and 3) Pray. You can be sure *"this is the will of God in Christ Jesus for you"* (1 Thessalonians 5:18). However, God's plans for you are much greater — if only you will seek Him for it. Consider these verses that show that God has a purpose for you.

1. **Ephesians 2:10:** *"For we are His workmanship, created in Christ Jesus for good works, which God prepared beforehand that we should walk in them."*
1. **Jeremiah 29:11-13:** *"For I know the thoughts that I think toward you, says the Lord, thoughts of peace and not of evil, to give you a future and a hope. Then you will call upon Me and go and pray to Me, and I will listen to you. And you will seek Me and find Me, when you search for Me with all your heart."*

You are very useful to God. Seek Him with your entire heart and wait for Him to reveal the good works that He has created especially for you. He will even use your afflictions to help others.

"Blessed be the God and Father of our Lord Jesus Christ, the Father of mercies and God of all comfort, who comforts us in all our tribulation, that we may be able to comfort those who are in any trouble, with the comfort with which we ourselves are comforted by God" (2 Corinthians 1:3-4).

-7. Cursed or Blessed?

Sometimes everything in life can seem to be working against you. Perhaps you've lost a job, home, or spouse. Your car has broken down, the refrigerator died, or the air conditioning is out. A string of what seems to be unfortunate events can cause you to think that perhaps God is against you. Maybe, you even feel cursed.

However, if you are in Christ, you are not cursed, but blessed. In fact, a curse cannot even come close to you (Proverbs 26:2). So long as you are living for Christ and repenting of sin, God is for you. You are blessed. Yet, God does use events that seem to be working against us as a means to accomplish something good for us. Never believe the lie that you are under a curse. If you are Christ's, you are blessed. Hold on to these promises from God to overcome this cord of false identity.

1. **Proverbs 3:33:** *"The curse of the Lord is on the house of the wicked, But He blesses the home of the just."*
2. **Proverbs 26:2:** *"Like a flitting sparrow, like a flying swallow, So a curse without cause shall not alight."*
3. **Psalm 1:1:** *"Blessed is the man who walks not in the counsel of the ungodly, nor stands in the path of sinners, nor sits in the seat of the scornful."*

God blesses the upright. If you are in Christ, no evil thing can come your way without God's permission. Never give Satan a foothold in your life by believing that you are cursed. *"And we know that all things work together for good to those who love God, to those who are the called according to His purpose"* (Romans 8:28).

Reclaiming Your True Identity

The key to reclaiming your true identity is to trust what God has to say about you. When someone is recovering from trauma or ungodly soul ties, it might be easier to believe the lies of the serpent than to trust in the true and living Word of Christ. However, we must break free from the cords of false identity if we want to have abundant, healthy relationships. Faith is the key.

"*So then faith comes by hearing, and hearing by the word of God*" (Romans 10:17). To build your faith, follow these five steps:

1. Immerse yourself in God's Word
2. Memorize pertinent verses
3. Believe the Scriptures
4. Respond in faith
5. Ask God to increase your faith

God delights to answer prayers that are in accordance with His will. If you follow the above five steps, you can be sure that He will increase your faith so that you can reclaim your true identity in Christ.

HOMEWORK

Answer the following questions:

1. What is the basis of your true identity?

2. Who is the author of your false identity?

3. Which cords of false identity do you need to cut off?

4. What verses can you begin memorizing to help cast off your cords of false identity?

5. What are the five steps you can take to reclaim your true identity?

6. Pray the prayers on the following page.

PRAYERS

1. Father, thank You that my true identity is defined by You.
2. Help me understand and believe my true identity.
3. I cast off all cords of false identity and refuse to believe the lies of the devil.
4. Help me overcome all cords of false identity in my life.
5. I am loved by God.
6. I am made whole in Christ.
7. I am fully accepted in the Beloved.
8. God has given me a sound mind.
9. In Christ, I am worthy and useful.
10. I am blessed with every spiritual blessing in Christ, who works all things out for my good. Amen.

DAY SEVEN

DECEPTIVE SELF-TALK

Finally, brethren, whatever things are true, noble, just, pure, lovely, [or] of good report, if there is any virtue and if there is anything praiseworthy—meditate on these things.
PHILIPPIANS 4:8

Have you ever paid attention to the conversations in your head? "I'm not good enough." "No one likes me." "God is against me." "I can't do it." "They are so much better than me." "I'll never be able to finish in time." "Why do I have to go through this?" "I've failed again." "I'll never change." "He hates me."

These cords of deceptive self-talk bind you to the lies of the devil. If you are recovering from ungodly soul ties and soul wounds, these are the very cords Satan can use to keep you from healing. You must break free. Yesterday we looked at some cords of false identity that can hold you in bondage. The next step is to break the habit of repeating the lies so you can start living in the truth. If you ever "hear" yourself repeating a lie about your identity, cut it off and speak the truth instead.

We will look at four categories of deceptive self-talk to help you break free from the cycle of bondage.

1. Lying About Yourself

Yesterday, we looked at seven truths about your identity. You are: Accepted; Beloved; Worthy; Whole; Bold; Useful; and Blessed. If you ever hear something in your mind that speaks to the contrary, you must stop the thought immediately and replace the lie with the truth.

Repeating something untrue about yourself violates the ninth commandment — even if you "feel" it is true. You cannot base truth on feelings. Instead, you must base all truth on the Word of God. "*Sanctify them by Your truth. Your word is truth*" (John 17:17). Satan is the father of lies. Don't listen to him.

If your mouth or mind says, "I'm not good enough," then replace it with a true statement like "God accepts me in Christ." Repeat the true phrase ten times if you must. Replace the wrong thought with the truth. Don't let Satan have control over your tongue or mind.

2. Lying About Circumstances

As Christians, "*We walk by faith, not by sight* (2 Corinthians 5:7). This means we must be especially careful to speak the truth about our circumstances. When things happen that seem bad or negative, it may "feel" natural to complain. Yet, we are commanded to "*Do all things without complaining or disputing*" (Philippians 2:14).

If Satan tempts us to say, "I'll never finish in time," we might respond instead with a more truthful statement. Here are some better options:

- "I may need more time to complete this project."
- "Is there anything I can do to work faster?"
- "With God's help, I will complete this on time."
- "I'll keep working until I'm finished."
- "What can I do next time to complete the project on schedule?"

When you feel negative emotions in your heart, you should be extra careful about your self-talk. If you are about to say something harmful, hurtful, or untruthful — stop. Find something good, lovely, and true to say instead. Satan loves to use our tongues for evil, but with God's help, we can overcome the devil's cords of negative self-talk.

3. Lying About Others

Another grave temptation is speaking lies in our hearts about others. Often, we act like God, reading the intentions of the hearts of our friends, family, or co-workers. However, if we are honest, we cannot read minds. We don't know what someone really intended.

If we hear our hearts say something like, "He hates me" or "She did that to hurt me," we are probably in league with the devil and bearing false witness in our hearts. Instead, we should think about others the way God requires. "*Let nothing be done through selfish ambition or conceit, but in lowliness of mind let each esteem others better than himself*" (Philippians 2:3).

An alternative to deceptive self-talk against others is to admit that you are not God and cannot read minds. You might pray for them or speak something true in your heart instead. Here are a few ideas:

- "Lord, help me forgive him for not being kind."
- "I wonder what is bothering her."
- "He must have had a really hard day."
- "Father, help me evaluate if I have done something to offend them."
- "Thank you, Lord, that my identity is found in how You think of me."

Remember the golden rule: do unto others as you would have them do unto you. We all stumble in many ways. It is always better to err on the side of grace. Sins of the tongue are set on fire by hell (James 3:6). Satan wants to keep us bound up with sin so we cannot achieve God's full blessings. Don't let the devil have his way with your tongue.

4. Lying About God

Perhaps the most grievous cord of deceptive self-talk is telling lies about God:

- "God doesn't love me."
- "God doesn't want me to have fun."
- "Obeying God is too hard."
- "God won't send anyone to hell."
- "Everything God does is against me."

Satan would like nothing better than to trick you into believing those lies about God. Anytime you hear your mouth (or mind) speak something contrary to God's Word, correct the lie immediately with Scripture. Here are some replacements for each deceptive cord above:

- "God loves me so much He died for me" (John 3:16).
- "God sent Jesus so I could live a more abundant life" (John 10:10).
- "I can do all things through Christ who strengthens me" (Philippians 4:13).
- "The cowardly, unbelieving, abominable, murderers, sexually immoral, sorcerers, idolaters, and all liars will have their part in the lake of fire" (Revelations 21:8).
- "God is working everything for my good" (Romans 8:28).

Satan has been a liar from the beginning. He loves to deceive people in order to keep them in bondage. You can break free from the cords of deceptive self-talk against God by speaking the truth of God's Word.

Speak the Truth

All cords of deceptive self-talk hold us in bondage to sin, Satan, and unhealthy relationships. We can always break free by speaking the truth in love. Consider this encouragement from David in Psalm 15:

> Lord, who may abide in Your tabernacle?
> Who may dwell in Your holy hill?
>
> He who walks uprightly,
> And works righteousness,
> And speaks the truth in his heart;
>
> He *who* does not backbite with his tongue,
> Nor does evil to his neighbor,
> Nor does he take up a reproach against his friend;
>
> In whose eyes a vile person is despised,
> But he honors those who fear the Lord;
> He *who* swears to his own hurt and does not change;
>
> He *who* does not put out his money at usury,
> Nor does he take a bribe against the innocent.
>
> He who does these *things* shall never be moved.

Be the person who walks uprightly and speaks the truth about yourself, your circumstances, your neighbor, and your God from the heart. If you do these things, you will never be moved.

HOMEWORK

Answer the following questions:

1. Which commandment do you violate when you engage in deceptive self-talk?

2. How does Satan use the cord of deceptive self-talk to keep you bound?

3. What are four categories of deceptive self-talk to beware of?

4. What is the solution to break free from the cords of deceptive self-talk?

5. List several alternatives to this deceptive self-talk: "I'm going to lose my job."

6. Pray the prayers on the following page.

PRAYERS

1. Father, purify my tongue.
2. Help me always speak the truth in love.
3. I cast off all cords of deceptive self-talk and choose to replace them with the truth.
4. Thank You, Jesus, for giving me the words of truth.
5. With Your help, I will only speak and think the truth about myself and others.
6. Forgive me for speaking lies against others in my heart.
7. Lord, I have often thought untruths about You. I confess and forsake that practice.
8. Increase my faith and trust in Your holy Word.
9. Father, I don't want my tongue to be set on fire by hell. Take the helm of my heart, Lord.
10. Help me walk uprightly, work righteousness, and speak the truth in my heart always, in Jesus' name.

DAY EIGHT

CORDS OF UNFORGIVINGNESS

Pursue peace with all people…looking carefully lest anyone fall short of the grace of God; lest any root of bitterness springing up cause trouble, and … many become defiled;
MATTHEW 6:15

We have been looking at the cords that keep us in bondage to ungodly soul ties. If we want to break free from all of Satan's tangles and webs, we must sever all cords of sin. These cords might be directly related to our previous unhealthy relationships, or they may stem from other heart issues. Sin is the root of all our bondages, even if the sin was not our own.

However, it often happens when another person sins against us, we further the sin by holding a grudge against them in our hearts. These grudges destroy healthy relationships. We must learn to let go of all bitterness and unforgivingness to escape the snare of the devil.

In future chapters, we will look more closely at unforgivingness and see that it is such a grievous sin that it puts us in danger of hellfire. For if we don't forgive others, God will not forgive us (Mark 11:26). Today, we are going to look at some very practical issues about what forgiveness looks like so Satan can't have any wiggle room in our lives, homes, and families.

What Is Forgiveness?

Forgiving someone means giving up some of the rights that we feel we have after someone has harmed us or sinned against us. Plus, it means taking some positive actions that show we have indeed forgiven the person. Sometimes forgiveness is a process. Let's look at five things we must not do and five things we must do when we forgive others. As you review these ten items, evaluate your heart to see if you are holding onto any unforgivingness against others.

5 Things Forgiveness Does Not Do

When you truly forgive someone from your heart, cutting all the cords of unforgivingness, you will no longer do the following:

1. **Hold a grudge:** Forgiving someone negates your right to hold a grudge in your heart against someone. That doesn't mean you have to allow them to hurt you again. That would not be wise. However, you must not hold hard feelings toward them.
2. **Dwell on the offense:** Forgiveness means that you stop rehashing the hurt over and over in your mind. You must practice positive self-talk, reminding yourself that you have forgiven the person and will not continue to think about the offense.
3. **Bring it up again:** Getting to the place of true forgiveness might include confronting a person with their offense. However, once forgiveness has occurred, you give up your right to mention the offense to the offending party in the future.
4. **Gossip about it with others:** You never have the right to gossip about another person. However, you may need counseling to work through forgiveness. Once forgiveness has occurred, you should not bring up the offense to anyone else again. If you are bringing it up, forgiveness has not truly occurred.
5. **Take vengeance:** While you never have the right to pay back someone evil for evil, the cords of unforgivingness might tempt you to do so. True forgiveness releases you from the temptation to retaliate wrong for wrong.

These steps are not always easy. You must rely upon the power of the Holy Spirit to help you forgive. But it is essential if you want to move on to future healthy relationships. Now, let's look at the five actions you must take in true forgiveness.

5 Marks of True Forgiveness

True forgiveness includes some action steps which might be difficult to take. However, it is vital that you take them. When you forgive someone, you agree that you will:

1. **Accept the consequences:** Accepting the consequences of a wrong done to you doesn't mean that you are agreeing that the consequences are fair. However, when you forgive, you acknowledge that there are consequences that you may have to live with. Perfect forgiveness would include receiving restitution for the wrong done. If restitution is

not possible, you must willingly accept the fallout of the harm done to you without bitterness.

2. **Show appropriate love to the offender:** The love you show to an offender will depend on the offense and the relationship of the offender. If you are forgiving your spouse, you must accept them again as your spouse, showing them the love God requires. However, if the offender sexually abused you as a child, the appropriate way to show love might be to turn them in to the authorities so they do not harm anyone else.
3. **Leave vengeance up to God:** Vengeance belongs to the Lord. He will repay evil-doers according to their deeds. The penalty might be through civil sanctions, divine judgment, or eternal damnation in hell. God may alternately choose to save the person, forgive their sin, and allow Jesus to pay the punishment. You must allow God to do what He deems just.
4. **Release negative emotions:** When you have been wronged, it often comes with anger, fear, sadness, bitterness, or hatred. These emotions are toxic to the soul. To forgive means to let go of these feelings. When they rise up in your soul, ask God to help you release them. We will deal more earnestly with negative emotions in further chapters.
5. **Enjoy the freedom:** Finally, when you have forgiven from the heart, you will experience true freedom in your soul. Satan will have no legal ground to torment you, and you will feel free to love God and others (including those who harmed you) without wounds in your soul. The result will be healthier relationships in the future.

Only a fool would say forgiveness is easy. Some wrongs are so painful, they seem impossible to let go of. This is when God gets to have the glory in your life. He can deliver you from unforgivingness and the ensuing pain.

Perhaps as you read through the 10 marks of forgiveness, you noticed you are holding on to bitterness toward someone who wronged you. Don't be dismayed. Continue working through forgiving others until you are completely free. We will broach the subject again. Tomorrow, we will begin to explore the source of ungodly soul ties and unhealthy relationships.

HOMEWORK

Answer the following questions:

1. What are five things you agree to forfeit when you forgive from your heart?

2. What are five things you agree to do when you forgive from your heart?

3. Why is it so vital to forgive others?

4. To whom does vengeance belong?

5. What are the ways that God can choose to repay someone who has hurt you?

6. Pray the prayers on the following page.

PRAYERS

1. Father, break me free from the cords of unforgivingness so I can enjoy healthy relationships.
2. Lord, it is so hard to forgive those who have harmed me.
3. Help me properly love and pray for those who have hurt me in any way.
4. When someone has violated me, help me not hold a grudge.
5. In forgiveness, teach me not to dwell on the painful memories.
6. Keep my lips from sinning by gossiping against those who have wronged me.
7. I give you all my anger, bitterness, clamor, and slander. Cleanse me, Lord.
8. Teach me to forgive from my heart.
9. Lord, remove all cords of unforgivingness in my life so I can be free.
10. Deliver me from every hurt, pain, injury, and trauma. I release them all to you, Lord, in Jesus' name.

DAY NINE

FOUNTAINS OF UNGODLY SOUL TIES

My people are destroyed for lack of knowledge.
HOSEA 4:6

As God is the fountain of all godly soul ties, sin, self, and Satan are the fountain of all ungodly soul ties. Over the next several chapters, we are going to look closer at some of the schemes the devil uses to deceive or force people to create negative soul ties and stay trapped in relationships that bring harm. Once we understand the tactics Satan uses, we can stop up the bitter fountains so the pure water can flow.

Sexual Sins and Ignorance

Today, we will look at two common fountains of ungodly soul ties: sexual sin and ignorance. Plus, we will share some ways to begin breaking these ties.

1. Illicit Sexual Intercourse

When you join your body together sexually outside of marriage, you create a spiritual bond that connects you to that person. *"Or do you not know that he who is joined to a harlot is one body with her? For 'the two,' He says, 'shall become one flesh'"* (1 Corinthians 6:16).

Since you become "one" in the sexual relationship, you are inviting the demons and sins that afflict the other party into your life. This is why 1 Corinthians 6:18 warns: *"Flee sexual immorality. Every sin that a man does is outside the body, but he who commits sexual immorality sins against his own body."* You do not want to invite another person's demons to take hold of you and influence you to do ungodly things.

One woman shares a story where she engaged in premarital sexual intercourse. Soon afterward, she started having thoughts outside of her control, making her say in her mind that she loved the devil. Later, she found out the man was demon-possessed. He had passed his demons onto her, and they tormented her until Christ delivered her.

Sexual intercourse outside of marriage introduces the transfer of demons from one person to another and can affect the mind, spirit, and behavior of the offenders. The demons seek to drag you further into sin, making it even more difficult to resist. All of God's ways are good. He has forbidden sex outside of marriage to protect people from this evil transference. If you are (or have been) involved in illicit sexual activity, you are bringing harm to your own body.

Ungodly soul ties from sexual sin can and must be broken. Start with these steps:

1. **Walk away** from these destructive behaviors and relationships.
2. **Seek deliverance** from any demonic activity that has resulted from the sin.
3. **Pray** for God to deliver you.

You will learn much more as you continue on your 40-day journey. But let's look at another scheme that Satan uses to hold people captive to ungodly soul ties.

Ignorance

Many people are unaware of the tactics that Satan uses to create ungodly soul ties. As a result, many Christians have an "open door" policy with the demonic realm and don't even know it. The result is difficult relationships, hardship, trauma, abuse, death, and other difficulties because they unknowingly attach themselves to people, objects, and ideas that negatively influence their life. This open-door policy not only contributes to ungodly soul ties, but also invites Satan and his minions into people's lives.

When people remain ignorant of the spiritual realm, they fail to take responsibility to stand firm against the wiles of the devil. Sometimes this ignorance comes from well-meaning, but unfruitful advice from pastors and other leaders. "Relax," they say. "The Lord defeated Satan, and he cannot hurt you anymore." This type of message can damage a believer's ability to protect themselves from Satan's evil plans. They look the other way while demons slip in the back door and begin to wreak havoc in their lives. Instead, Christians ought to heed the instructions of the

Apostle Paul who said, *"Put on the whole armor of God, that you may be able to stand against the wiles of the devil"* (Ephesians 6:11).

We must take every lawful means to discover the schemes of Satan so that we do not ignorantly allow demons to cause mayhem in our lives. The best spiritual warfare manual is the Bible. We should know it inside and out so we can stand firm against Satan's ploys to kill, steal, and destroy. Plus, as we study and memorize Scripture, we can claim the promises and power of God and plead the blood of Christ. There are myriads of principles from Genesis to Revelation to guide you. Here are a few steps to get started.

1. **Study the Word of God** like your life depends upon it.
2. **Memorize Scriptures** that reveal Satan's schemes and how to fight them.
3. **Pray continually** for God to grant you wisdom and understanding.

Sexual immorality and ignorance are two fountains of ungodly soul ties that must be squashed. If you struggle with sexual immorality of any kind (pornography, promiscuity, adultery, masturbation, homosexuality, bestiality, cross-dressing, gender confusion, etc.), you can be sure there is a demon behind it. Yet, God has the power to break these strongholds in your life and bring you total deliverance.

Tomorrow, we are going to dive into ungodly relationships to see how they lead to destructive behavior, sin, and demonic control in your life.

HOMEWORK

Answer the following questions:

1. Why does God warn against sexual sin in the Bible?

2. Do you have any sexual sins to confess and forsake?

3. What steps can you take to prevent future sexual sins in your life?

4. What is an "open door" policy with the demonic realm? Do you have one?

5. How often do you read your Bible? If you are not doing so already, begin reading it daily.

6. Pray the prayers on the following page.

PRAYERS

1. Father, keep me pure from sexual sin and ignorance.
2. I reject all forms of sexual sins.
3. Don't let Satan have a foothold in my life.
4. Break me free from all ungodly soul ties.
5. Thank You for godly soul ties.
6. Give me a hunger and thirst for Your Word.
7. Don't let my ignorance of Satan's scheme hold me in bondage.
8. Help me study to show myself approved.
9. I want to live without bondage to sin, self, and Satan.
10. Set me free to experience total freedom in relationships.

DAY TEN

UNGODLY RELATIONSHIPS

Do not be deceived: "Evil company corrupts good habits."
1 Corinthians 15:33

Lot was a man that was counted among the righteous. Yet, the Apostle Peter says that his righteous soul was tormented day to day because he lived among the unrighteous people of Sodom and Gomorrah (2 Peter 2:6-8). It was a choice to live among wicked men, and it led to more than torment in his soul. Lot's soul ties with an ungodly culture led to compromise, sin, and destruction.

In His mercy, God sent angels to rescue Lot from the pending judgment on Sodom and Gomorrah. The city was so wicked that the men of the town sought to sodomize the angels that were sent to rescue Lot from destruction. Lot offered his daughters to the wicked men instead. The angels intervened and literally pulled Lot and his family from their home to escape God's judgment. Lot's wife was unwilling to break the ties. She was so "connected" to the city that she disobeyed God and was turned into a pillar of salt. But there is more.

Lot had betrothed his two daughters to godless men in the city. Since the fiancees did not believe there was a pending destruction, they died in the fire and brimstone. And to make matters worse, Lot's two daughters got Lot drunk in order to lie with him carnally so they could bear children through their father. Two sons were born to Lot through incest.

These spurious events were the result of Lot's compromise through ungodly soul ties with unbelievers. We must guard against forming relationships and alliances with wicked men. Today, we will look at ungodly relationships and how they open doorways to demonic soul ties. Plus, we will share some ways to begin breaking these ties so you can live in the total freedom that Christ purchased for you. Don't compromise with ungodly relationships as Lot did.

Soul Ties Through Ungodly Relationships

When you choose to have a relationship with an unbeliever (knowingly or unknowingly), you open yourself up to ungodly soul ties. As you bond with them, it opens doorways for their familiar spirits, sins, and demons to invade your life. Perhaps you've noticed how when people hang out together long enough, they start to act and think alike. 1 Corinthians 15:33 explains why: *"Do not be deceived: "Evil company corrupts good habits."* You are fooling yourself if you believe you can have close friendships with godless people and walk away unharmed. Remember Lot.

Examine every current relationship and every past relationship that has broken apart in your life for any reason. This includes relationships within your family, friendship circles, the business world, or of any nature. If there was any kind of sin involved in these relationships or you have knit your heart with an unbeliever, there is the potential that it left behind an unfruitful soul tie. These bonds of negativity have thorns that should be cast away. *"But evil men are all to be cast aside like thorns, which are not gathered with the hand"* (2 Samuel 23:6 NIV).

We are not to be knit together with those who are in the darkness. *"For what fellowship has righteousness with lawlessness? And what communion has light with darkness? And what accord has Christ with Belial? Or what part has a believer with an unbeliever?"* (2 Corinthians 6:14-15).

Break the Ungodly Ties

You must sever these soul ties in the physical and the spiritual world. Breaking them now can save you a world of trouble. You don't want to be like Lot who lost his wife to the world, compromised his integrity, and brought misfortune to his future kin.

Physical Break

A physical break might include breaking off a friendship, leaving a romantic relationship, moving out of the home you share with an unbeliever, biblically divorcing an unfaithful spouse, breaking a business relationship, quitting a job that is asking you to lie, selling your share in joint property with an unbeliever, or any other breaking of a relationship that is causing you to sin or compromise.

However, after the physical break, the soul tie may still remain. You must take action to break the spiritual and emotional bond as well. Lot's wife broke off the physical tie by leaving the city, but her heart was still so closely knit to it that she lost her life. Cut the vine that ties the two of you together so you can move on and enjoy a separate and healthy life.

Spiritual Break

Only God can break a spiritual or emotional soul tie. Ask God to remove any demonic connections related to the relationship. Use self-control to stop thinking about the person or relationship. If you find your mind wandering back to the person or relationship, fall on your knees and cry out to God for help.

Every night before you go to sleep, take some time and energy in thought and prayer cutting the ungodly ties that still linger in your soul. This can help you relax and sleep better since stress and difficulty sleeping are often symptoms of ungodly soul ties. Be prepared to stay up until God has brought to mind all the people you are tied to negatively. Ask God the Holy Spirit to guide your mind so you do not leave any ungodly bonds open. During times of intense spiritual warfare against demonic influences, this practice is especially important as these bonds can make you impotent against the powers of darkness.

Do what it takes to sever the ungodly ties. Release all negativity from your spirit, and you will sleep more comfortably. Plus, you will experience more freedom in all areas of your life. Past ungodly relationships can prevent you from experiencing the fullness of joy that is available to those who abide in Christ.

HOMEWORK

Answer the following questions:

1. In what ways did Lot's compromise lead to sin, destruction, and harm?

2. Why do people in close relationships start acting alike?

3. What current or past relationships are leading you to (or have led you to) compromise?

4. What steps can you take to sever these ties physically and spiritually?

5. List any emotional ties that still linger after a physical break. How can you break these?

6. Pray the prayers on the following page.

PRAYERS

1. Father, I don't want to compromise like Lot.
2. Please break all ungodly soul ties in my life.
3. Help me to break of ungodly relationships that are leading me to sin.
4. Destroy the emotional and spiritual bonds of all ungodly soul ties.
5. Protect me from the evil schemes of Satan to hold me in bondage.
6. Do not let evil company corrupt my habits.
7. Remove Satan's foothold in my life.
8. Father, bring to mind all ungodly soul ties so I can break their power in my life for harm.
9. Please bring godly relationships into my life so I can experience the fullness of Your joy.
10. Grant me total freedom from all ungodly relationships and soul ties.

DAY ELEVEN

UNGODLY TIES WITH BELIEVERS

But now I have written to you not to keep company with anyone named a brother who is sexually immoral.
1 Corinthians 5:11

In the last chapter, we discussed the need to be careful with close-knit relationships with ungodly men and women. And while it is true that *"evil company corrupts good habits"* (1 Corinthians 15:33) — there is a place for these relationships in the Christian's life. We must balance everything according to the full counsel of God.

In 1 Corinthians 5:9-10, the Apostle Paul writes, *"I wrote to you in my epistle not to keep company with sexually immoral people. Yet I certainly did not mean with the sexually immoral people of this world, or with the covetous, or extortioners, or idolaters, since then you would need to go out of the world."* We cannot avoid all relationships with ungodly people. In fact, we ought to have relationships with outsiders so we can bring them to the saving knowledge of Jesus Christ. However, we must be careful not to use our friendships as a cover for sin, nor create ungodly soul ties with unbelievers that could lead to the warnings listed in the previous chapter.

Interestingly, Paul provides a more stern warning to Christians about having close relationships and associations with other Christians who are engaged in blatant sin. And that's what we will discuss more deeply in this chapter.

Christians Who Lack Love

Ungodly soul ties do not only stem from inappropriate relationships with unbelievers; they can also form in relationships with professing and true believers. If you are in a close relationship with a Christian who does not love God and neighbor properly, you may need to sever that relationship for your own protection and their healing. Below are some examples.

1. **Sins Against You:** "*We all stumble in many things*" (James 3:2). Yet, when your brother or sister in Christ stumbles in a way that harms you, you have an obligation to confront them with their sin. If they refuse to listen, you are not to associate with that person. "*Moreover if your brother sins against you, go and tell him his fault between you and him alone. If he hears you, you have gained your brother. But if he will not hear, take with you one or two more, that 'by the mouth of two or three witnesses every word may be established.' And if he refuses to hear them, tell it to the church. But if he refuses even to hear the church, let him be to you like a heathen and a tax collector*" (Matthew 18:15-17).

2. **Egregious Sins:** The Apostle Paul also warns believers not to associate with "so-called" Christians who engage in specific egregious sins. "*But now I have written to you not to keep company with anyone named a brother, who is sexually immoral, or covetous, or an idolater, or a reviler, or a drunkard, or an extortioner—not even to eat with such a person*" (1 Corinthians 5:11). It can be extremely difficult to sever soul ties with believing friends, but in these cases, it is vital for your spiritual health and even the salvation of the other person (1 Corinthians 5:5). If we do not sever the tie, we may be subject to the same demonic influences that are holding these believers in bondage.

3. **Lack of Love:** Christians are to be knit together with cords of love. Lack of love in a godly relationship creates discord between family members, church members, and Christian friends, destroying true unity and peace. When godly love is missing in godly relationships, the results are quite negative, resulting in anger, hate, resentment, jealousy, conflict, and more. We are commanded to break away from these ties in a godly fashion. "*Cast out the scoffer, and contention will leave; Yes, strife and reproach will cease*" (Proverbs 22:10).

    A positive relationship with godly believers will produce true love and the fruit of the Spirit, even "*love, joy, peace, long-suffering, kindness, goodness, faithfulness, gentleness, self-control*" (Galatians 5:22).

4. **Walking in the Flesh:** We are also warned against walking according to the lusts of the flesh. We must not fellowship with believers who give in to baser interests, lustful thoughts, and impurity, creating idols in their hearts and minds. Plus, we must guard our own hearts against these things.

Guard also against those who demonstrate jealousy, gossip, anger, self-promotion, critical judging, fault-finding, pride, egotistical attitudes, and self-seeking. These harmful attributes can easily be passed along to you through the spirit realm or by habit, and they do not align with God's directives for life. Do not form close bonds with people displaying these behaviors. Warn them in love when possible.

Two believers can only come together with a loving bond when they live at peace with God and in joy with each other, seeking the needs of each other first.

Since none of us are without sin, we need to navigate these waters with great wisdom, lest we cast a stone that bruises us. We must break from these ties with great caution, looking first to our own sins so that we do not cast fault inappropriately and fall into the sin of pride. Prayerfully consider the following verses before engaging in this kind of spiritual warfare:

- **Matthew 7:3-5:** *"And why do you look at the speck in your brother's eye, but do not consider the plank in your own eye? Or how can you say to your brother, 'Let me remove the speck from your eye'; and look, a plank is in your own eye? Hypocrite! First remove the plank from your own eye, and then you will see clearly to remove the speck from your brother's eye."*
- **2 Timothy 2:24-26:** *"And a servant of the Lord must not quarrel but be gentle to all, able to teach, patient, in humility correcting those who are in opposition, if God perhaps will grant them repentance, so that they may know the truth, and that they may come to their senses and escape the snare of the devil, having been taken captive by him to do his will."*
- **Galatians 6:1:** *"Brethren, if a man is overtaken in any trespass, you who are spiritual restore such a one in a spirit of gentleness, considering yourself lest you also be tempted."*
- **1 Peter 4:8:** *"And above all things have fervent love for one another, for 'love will cover a multitude of sins.'"*

Let us not break fellowship over petty differences and the opinions of men. Rather, let's follow the biblical instructions of when to break ties with believers in light of the verses given above on how to confront the sins of a brother. Above all, seek the favor of God in all things. *"The fear of man brings a snare, But whoever trusts in the Lord shall be safe"* (Proverbs 29:25).

HOMEWORK

Answer the following questions:

1. Under what grounds can you have relationships with unbelievers?

2. How does God want you to treat other Christians who are caught in sin?

3. Do you have any ungodly soul ties with believers?

4. What steps can you take to sever these ties physically and spiritually?

5. Explain the manner you ought to confront sin in a believer's life?

6. Pray the prayers on the following page.

PRAYERS

1. Father, help me not to associate with Christians who are engaged in sin.
2. Give me the wisdom to know which sins to cover with love and which sins to make a clean break from.
3. I will not keep company with a Christian brother who is sexually immoral.
4. When someone sins against me, help me confront them in love.
5. Help me find Christian friends who know how to demonstrate Christian love.
6. Let me be a friend who genuinely loves others according to Your Word.
7. Guard me against friends who are jealous, gossips, angry, self-promoting, critical judgers, fault-finders, proud, egotistical, and self-seeking.
8. Keep these sins far from me.
9. Help me never break fellowship over petty differences and the opinions of men.
10. Show me the relationships I need to break, in Jesus' name.

DAY TWELVE

GENERATIONAL SOUL TIES

He by no means clears the guilty, visiting the iniquity of the fathers on the children to the third and fourth generation.
NUMBERS 14:8

Today, we will look at generational sin. The fountain of this ungodly soul tie is outside the control of the one afflicted. In fact, generational sin began in the Garden of Eden. All humans inherit a "sin nature" from our first father, Adam, and are under a curse of death. Thankfully, when we trust Christ, we become part of the family of God. And through the blood of Christ, we overcome the curse of death and have power over our sinful nature. This is how we can break free from generational sins.

God is a promise keeper. And Satan knows this full well. Though the devil must work within the framework that God has established, he will use every advantage to influence people for harm. God has promised that He will "visit" the iniquities of the children to the third and fourth generations. This gives Satan freedom to send his demonic forces against our children and grandchildren when we have unconfessed sin.

If you are involved in any sin, you should be thinking about how that sin will affect your future generations. Do you want your children involved in pornography, drunkenness, slander, hatred, lying, stealing, thieving, and the like? Turn from those sins now, and ask God to break the generational curse through the blood of Jesus.

Case Study #1

A woman tells the story of a generational curse she experienced as a child in the sixth grade. At that age, she was starting to notice boys and was concerned about her bodily image. However, she also really liked food, and didn't want to cut back.

One day, sitting on her back steps, an idea came to her mind. She thought, "If I just throw up my food, I can eat and stay skinny." Without sticking her finger down her throat or making any effort, she was able to purge her meal and flush it down the toilet.

This behavior went on for years. One day, she noticed that her mother's hands smelled like vomit and asked her why. The mother confessed to sticking her finger down her throat so she could vomit her food to stay slim.

Because the (believing) mother, was engaged in the sin of binging and purging (often wrongly diagnosed as an illness called bulimia), the sin was passed on to the daughter even though she had no idea that her mother was involved in that same sin.

Eventually, both mother and daughter confessed the behavior as sin and stopped the practice. God completely delivered them from this godless behavior that was inspired by demons.

It is important to note that the mother ultimately was not responsible for the behavior of the daughter, nor were the demons. The daughter willingly gave in to the sin rather than resisting. The Bible says, *"Resist the devil and he will flee from you"* (James 4:7). While generational sins give Satan permission to tempt us; we have the power to resist in Christ.

Resist the Devil

Because there are often demons involved in generational sins, they can be difficult to resist. However, we can and must resist them in the power of Jesus Christ.

Consider the actions of your father, mother, and grandparents on both sides going back to four generations. Do you notice any similar sinful patterns that have emerged in your life? While some of these can be learned by example, they often have behind them the power of demons.

An unregenerate (unsaved) person, will not be able to resist these demonic forces. Children can be especially vulnerable. If you have children who have not shown forth the testimony or the fruits of salvation, cover them in prayer daily as Job did for his children. *"Job would send and sanctify them, and he would rise early in the morning and offer burnt offerings according to the number of them all. For Job said, 'It may be that my sons have sinned and cursed God in their hearts.' Thus Job did regularly"* (Job 1:5).

Job's prayers for his children set a hedge about them that Satan could not break through. *"Have You not made a hedge around him, around his household, and around all that he has on every side?"* (Job 1:10). However, if we regard iniquity in our hearts, we should not expect God to protect our children from the wiles of Satan.

Case Study #2

A single mother, newly converted to the Lord, witnessed her one-year-old daughter rocking back and forth on the bed. The estranged father had a history with pornography and masturbation. It became evident to the mother that the small child was masturbating, which she didn't even think was possible for a child of such a young age.

There were no signs of sexual abuse, yet the child displayed behaviors that could only be explained through generational sins. As the child grew older, the mother also found herself tempted toward "self-fulfillment." However, the mother started to notice that whenever she felt the urge to masturbate, she would find her daughter involved in the same behavior in a different room. Finally, the mother saw the connection between her own sinful lusts and the behavior of her child. Through prayer, confession, and turning from sin, both mother and daughter were delivered from the demonic influences.

Whenever the mother was tempted to sin, she thought of her daughter's condition above her own. She did not want to allow Satan the opportunity to drag her young daughter into sin.

Breaking Generational Sins

Understanding how generational sins work through the spiritual realm can help you break free from the destructive consequences. In Christ, we can break free from generational sins through the promises in the Bible. *"Therefore, if anyone is in Christ, he is a new creation; old things have passed away; behold, all things have become new"* (2 Corinthians 5:17).

The first step is to confess your sin and accept your new life in Christ. Then, turn from your sins in the power of Christ's resurrection. Finally, resist the devil and he will flee from you. Jesus came to destroy the works of the devil. Praise His name! This is what the gospel of Jesus is all about. The gospel is such an important topic, we are going to learn why we need to preach it to ourselves daily. But that's tomorrow's task. Today, we've got some homework to attend to.

HOMEWORK

Answer the following questions:

1. What is the power behind generational sins? And how can you break it?

2. Why did God put a hedge of protection around Job's children?

3. List any generational sins in your family heritage.

4. Renounce and turn from any generational sins that are holding you in bondage.

5. Are there any sins in your life that you are in danger of passing on to your children and grandchildren? Confess them today.

6. Pray the prayers on the following page.

PRAYERS

1. Father, I know I am a sinner. I don't want to pass my sins on to my children. Cleanse me of all unrighteousness.
2. Protect my children and future generations from the sins of their fathers.
3. Teach me to resist the devil with all power and authority.
4. Thank You for protecting me and my children from the evil one.
5. I plead the blood of Jesus on my life and the life of my family against all demonic spirits and strongholds from generational sins.
6. Lord, show me sins in my life that I need to confess and forsake.
7. Grant me total deliverance from all ungodly soul ties established through inheritance.
8. Cleanse my bloodline, Lord.
9. Father, thank You for adopting me into Your family.
10. Thank you, Lord, for making all things new.

DAY THIRTEEN

FREEDOM FROM THE CURSE OF THE LAW

Christ has redeemed us from the curse of the law, having become a curse for us.
GALATIANS 3:13

How well do you know the gospel? It is the power of God to overcome the evil one, break ungodly soul ties, and enjoy healthy relationships. Without the gospel, we cannot love God, turn from sin, or love others the way we ought. Satan knows the gospel can set us free, and he would like nothing more than to keep us ignorant of its mighty power. The devil would much prefer to hold us captive to sin, guilt, and shame, the very things that foster broken relationships.

A wise man once said, "Preach the gospel to yourself daily. Preach it to the devil if you must." In order to preach the gospel to ourselves and the devil, we must understand it inside and out — it is our power for deliverance from that ancient foe and all his ploys. *"For I am not ashamed of the gospel of Christ, for it is the power of God to salvation for everyone who believes, for the Jew first and also for the Greek"* (Romans 1:16).

What Is the Gospel?

The good news of Jesus Christ is often shrouded in a word that has little meaning today: gospel. The word originally derives from the Greek word εὐαγγέλιον, which according to Strong's Concordance, literally means "a good message" or "to announce good news." Later, the word was translated as "godspell" which meant "good story." We must always think of the gospel as good news and as a good (true) story because that's what it is. Let's look at seven basic components of the gospel, which have everything to do with Christ:

1. **Death:** Christ died for our sins.

2. **Burial:** He was buried in the tomb.
3. **Resurrection:** Christ rose from the grave.
4. **Ascension:** He ascended into heaven.
5. **Exaltation:** He sat down at the right hand of God.
6. **Reign:** He is ruling from heaven until all His enemies are a footstool for His feet
7. **Return:** He will return to earth, raise the dead, and destroy His last enemy, death.

These components of the gospel are wonderful. Yet, in order to really understand what makes this such good news, we need to look a little deeper.

What Makes the Gospel so Good?

After Adam and Eve sinned, God pronounced a curse of death upon the entire world. Every man, woman, and child is born under this curse of death, including you. Plus, each one of us participates in the curse by choosing to sin: *"For all have sinned and fall short of the glory of God"* (Romans 3:23). The Bible reminds us that *"the wages of sin is death"* (Romans 6:23). Whether from Adam's sin or our own, we all deserve death. *"There is none righteous, no, not one"* (Romans 3:10).

Even if we tried our hardest to please God and live for Him, we would still fall short of His perfect standard. *"But we are all like an unclean thing, and all our righteousnesses are like filthy rags"* (Isaiah 64:6). You see: God is holy. He cannot tolerate sin, nor overlook it. There is nothing we can do to live up to His righteous standards or reverse the curse of death. We are all bound under sin and deserve hell. These are just the facts. You may not feel or believe that you are bound by sin and deserve hell, but it's true. And there is absolutely nothing you can do to save yourself from this predicament. You are born under God's curse of death (the curse of the Law).

You may be wondering, "I thought the gospel is good news; this sounds pretty bad." And it is bad. If you don't know how bad your situation really is before God, you will never be able to understand why the gospel is so beautiful. *"For the wages of sin is death,* **but the gift of God is eternal life in Christ Jesus our Lord**" (Romans 6:23).

How Do You Receive the Gift?

The only way to receive the gift of life is through grace, mercy, and faith. *"But God, who is rich in **mercy**, because of His great love with which He loved us, even when we were dead in trespasses, made us alive together with Christ (by grace you have been saved), and raised us up together, and made us sit together in the heavenly places in Christ Jesus, that in the ages to come He might show the exceeding riches of His grace in His kindness toward us in Christ Jesus. For by **grace** you have been saved through **faith**, and that not of yourselves; it is the gift of God, not of works, lest anyone should boast"* (Ephesians 2:4-8).

All you must do to receive the gift of eternal life is to obey what Christ taught: *"Repent, and believe in the gospel"* (Mark 1:15). To repent is to agree with God that you are a sinner, ask God to forgive you, and "turn" away from your sin. To believe the gospel means that you acknowledge:

1. You are a sinner, under the curse of death, and unable to save yourself.
2. God sent His Son Jesus Christ into the world to save sinners like you.
3. Jesus, God in the flesh, lived a sinless life, and died on your behalf, paying the penalty of death that you deserved.
4. Because Christ was undeserving of death, He resurrected from the dead.
5. Many days later, Christ ascended into heaven and sat down at the right hand of power.
6. In Christ, God sees you as perfect and holy, as though you have perfectly obeyed God's commandments and never sinned.
7. When you die, you will spend eternity with God and Christ in heaven along with all those who have trusted in Christ ALONE for their salvation.

After repenting and believing the gospel, you are free from the curse of the Law. Death has no power over you. But there is one more step you must take to remain free from the grip of Satan and the consequences of sin. You must perfectly obey all of the commandments of God. And this too is impossible. But as always, God has the solution: preach the gospel to yourself daily.

Your Greatest Weapon

Even after repenting of sin and believing the gospel, we all continue to sin daily. *"If we say we have no sin, we deceive ourselves, and the truth is not in us"* (1 John 1:8). Since sin is the very thing that opens us up to harmful relationships and the attacks of Satan, what can we do? The answer is of course in the Bible: "*If we confess our sins, He is faithful and just to forgive us our sins and to cleanse us from all unrighteousness*" (1 John 1:9).

The greatest weapon against disobedience is to preach the gospel to yourself daily, confessing and turning from your sin continually. Salvation is a one-time event. Repentance is an ongoing practice that leads to sanctification (where we become more like Christ).

Genuine repentance breaks the power of Satan in your life and sets the stage for healthy relationships. Repent often, remembering that Christ paid for your sins, which means your soul is secure. Satan cannot touch you without God's permission. With the good news of Jesus Christ abiding in your heart, you have the power to form godly and eternal relationships.

Do you believe the good news? You are going to need it as we continue to expose the corruptions that keep us bound to ungodly soul ties and toxic relationships. Tomorrow, we're going to dive into the super glue of soul ties: addictions.

HOMEWORK

Answer the following questions:

1. Explain the gospel. What makes it so good?

2. Have you repented of your sins and believed the gospel?

3. What are the consequences of ignoring the gospel?

4. What does it mean to be free from the curse of the Law?

5. What must you do daily to stay free from the curses of sin?

6. Pray the prayers on the following page.

PRAYERS

1. Father, I am a sinner deserving of death.
2. Thank You for sending Jesus Christ to take the penalty I deserve for my sin.
3. Apart from Christ, all my righteousness is as filthy rags.
4. Cleanse me of my sins, Lord.
5. You have freed me from the curse of the Law; sin and death have no power over me.
6. Thank You for being faithful and just to forgive my sins and cleanse me of all unrighteousness.
7. Help me live more and more for You so I can establish healthy, eternal relationships.
8. Thank You, Lord, for your gift of salvation.
9. I see, Lord, I can do nothing to gain Your favor but to believe.
10. Help me to remember daily to preach the gospel to myself.

DAY FOURTEEN

THE SUPER GLUE OF SOUL TIES

*And do not be conformed to this world, but be transformed
by the renewing of your mind.*
ROMANS 12:2

During sexual relations, winning at gambling, drug use, or even after eating chocolate, our brain releases a natural chemical called dopamine. This "feel good" chemical affects many aspects of our lives and can have both positive and negative effects. And there's a little problem: Our brain and body do not differentiate between dopamine that comes from illicit sex, candy, or exercise. When a person chooses a drug or unhealthy stimulant — or engages in sinful "feel good" activities — it forms bonds that lead to addiction.

Dopamine-releasing activities activate a super-glue-like bond whether we want them to or not. Sinful behaviors and sexual relationships, both chosen and nonconsensual, can trigger an ongoing force of unwanted emotions, thoughts, and habits that may not be linked to pleasure, but still come from those automatic chemical reactions in the body. Addictive soul ties can form around relationships, substances, or activities. For total healing from addictions, you must dissolve any super glue that has you stuck to you through ungodly soul ties.

Addictive Relationships

Healthy relationships are built on biblical love, trust, and freedom. Evaluate the following questions to see if you have a soul tie to a relationship that is addictive.

1. Do you constantly hear a person's thoughts in your head?
2. Do you often mull over past interactions and conversations?
3. Are you continually thinking about that person throughout the day?

4. Are your nighttime dreams or nightmares focused on that individual or circumstance?
5. Do you image someone else while engaged in regular relations with your spouse?

If you are experiencing any of these symptoms, you may need to break free from the addictive relationship.

Addictive Substances

Below are some questions to ask to help you evaluate if you have a soul tie with a substance like alcohol, drugs, food, or any other item that releases dopamine in your brain.

1. Do you focus on how you are going to get your next drink, dose, or bite?
2. Are you hiding your behavior from those you love?
3. Do you make decisions based on how it will affect your chances of using or consuming the substance?
4. Would you say NO to spending time with family, friends, and other believers so you could have access to the substance?
5. Do you dream about the substance regularly?

If you answer yes to one or more of these questions, you may have a super-glue bond to the substance that needs to be broken by the power of God. Addictions destroy more than relationships.

Addictive Activities

Sinful and non-sinful activities can also be addictive. Sex, TV, exercise, extreme sports, hoarding, video games, music, phone time, racing, crafts, and other activities that cause you to have an emotional response, could have an addictive nature if not subdued by the Spirit of God. Below are some questions to ask yourself in light of your activities.

1. Why do you do the activity?
2. How much time do you spend engaging in the activity?
3. Are you neglecting a godly relationship because of the activity?
4. Could you go a day, week, or month without it?
5. Does the activity break any commandments of God or laws of the land?

6. Is your affection for the thing growing out of control?
7. Does the activity glorify God?

Just because you enjoy an activity does not make it wrong. However, if you are choosing the activity outside of the will of God or instead of fulfilling God-given obligations (like work, kindness to others, cooking dinner, caring for your children, etc.), the activity could be an idol in your life, causing a demonic soul tie that will make it difficult to maintain healthy relationships.

Create New Pathways

When our brain releases dopamine (a God-given process), we have the desire to experience the feeling again. This can work for our good if we are engaged in healthy, God-ordained activities. However, if our brain makes our body "feel good" with sin, we will also desire to repeat these sinful activities. If we give in to our sinful desires, our brain builds neural pathways making us want to engage more and more in the activity. Soon, we think of nothing else. We are addicted.

To break this sinful cycle, we need to create new pathways in the brain. When we do, the Bible tells us we can be transformed. It starts by renewing the mind.

*"I beseech you therefore, brethren, by the mercies of God, that you present your bodies a living sacrifice, holy, acceptable to God, which is your reasonable service. And do not be conformed to this world, but **be transformed by the renewing of your mind**, that you may prove what is that good and acceptable and perfect will of God"* (Romans 12:2).

How To Break the Bond

Below is a list of steps you can take to start loosening the super glue that's holding your negative soul ties together.

1. **Renew Your Mind:** Study the Word of God and memorize Scripture passages that tell you what is right, what is wrong, and what the consequences are for doing right and wrong. This will start weakening the old pathways.
2. **Conform to Christ:** Now that you know what God requires, start practicing it even if it feels uncomfortable or even hurts. This will start creating new pathways.
3. **Take Off and Put On:** Think about your addiction. What is it costing you? Relationships, health, time with family, money, sleep, life? Imagine yourself taking off the habit and putting on the thing that you are losing.

4. **Pray without Ceasing:** You can do nothing apart from Christ. Ask Him to fill you with His power to overcome and to remove the demonic soul ties that keep you in bondage.
1. **Stay Accountable:** Find godly friends that you can trust. Ask them to pray for you. Tell them about your struggles. Meet with them regularly to discuss your successes and failures.

Start applying these steps to your life to break free from the super glue that is holding you captive. Before moving on to the homework, there is one more issue to address.

At Higher Risk

Have you ever noticed that two people can be exposed to the same temptation but respond completely differently? Some people are more prone to addiction. If you have been abused as a child; raped; tortured; unloved; suffered tragedy; experienced severe trauma; lost a loved one; gone through hardship, etc., then you may be more susceptible to addiction.

If this is you, seek out a compassionate biblical counselor who can help you work through and heal from your trauma. God's Word does have the answers for all these things. You too can be renewed. Never give up hope. As long as you are fighting for freedom, expect that God is fighting for you. Plus, make sure to continue working through this book as it is loaded with helpful means to experience total freedom.

HOMEWORK

Answer the following questions:

1. List any relationships, activities, or substances in your life that border on addiction.

2. How do the chemical reactions in the brain help super-glue you to addictive behaviors?

3. What are five steps you can take to break free from these bonds?

4. How do you create new pathways in your brain?

5. If you have been abused or traumatized, seek out biblical counsel.

6. Pray the prayers on the following page.

PRAYERS

1. Father, release me from all ungodly soul ties formed from chemical reactions in my brain.
2. I reject all sinful behavior and choose to walk in the light of Your Word.
3. Christ, Your blood has the power to break the strongest bonds.
4. I cry to You, Lord, to break all bonds of addiction in my life.
5. Transform me, Lord, by renewing my mind.
6. Conform me to Your image, Lord.
7. I present my body to you as a living sacrifice, holy, acceptable to God, which is my reasonable service.
8. Father, help me seek out godly friends to keep me accountable.
9. Remove every satanic soul tie that seeks to keep me glued to sin, in Jesus' name.
10. Thank You, Lord, for never giving up on me, in Jesus' name.

DAY FIFTEEN

DIGGING DEEPER INTO RELATIONSHIPS

Test all things; hold fast what is good.
Abstain from every form of evil.
1 Thessalonians 5:21-22

We have covered a lot of ground over the past two weeks. Today we are going to engage in some more self-evaluation. First, we will ask a series of questions that will help you further determine if you have any ungodly soul ties affecting the relationships in your life. Then, we will ask some questions to help you evaluate the godly soul ties in your life. The goal of this chapter is to fulfill the admonition of 1 Thessalonians 5:21-22: *"Test all things; hold fast what is good. Abstain from every form of evil."*

Testing for Ungodly Soul Ties

As you read through these questions, be honest with yourself. You can hide nothing from God. Simply answer "yes" or "no" (tests don't get any easier than that).

1. Do you have trouble forgiving people who have hurt or wronged you or someone else?
2. Are you regularly frustrated or angry when people get away with hurting you or others?
3. Does your love for a significant other keep you tied to a relationship even when they treat you very badly?
4. Have you experienced physical, emotional, or sexual abuse in any relationship but don't want to walk away from the abuser?
5. Are you having difficulty letting go of a relationship after a break-up or loss?
6. Have you experienced more than one relationship in the past that you would consider toxic?
7. Did you fail to effectively deal with and move on from a physical or emotional pain caused by another person in your past?

8. Do you feel like the people who hurt you are the only ones who will ever want you?
9. Have you returned to a toxic relationship even though you knew it was wrong?
10. Do you struggle with the fear that your partner will abandon you?
11. Do you feel that you must constantly prove to others that you are worthy to be loved?
12. Do you believe your relationships depend on you proving something to others?

If you have answered any of these questions in the affirmative, your life will be negatively influenced by these bonds. Do not let this trouble you. These ungodly soul ties can be destroyed. The first step to healing is always recognizing the problem. In the next chapter, we will provide some keys to start removing them from your life for good (with the Lord's help). Now, let's test the godly soul ties in your life.

Testing for Godly Soul Ties

As you read through these questions, you should again answer with a simple "yes" or "no".

1. Have all of your relationships existed without physical, sexual, or emotional abuse?
2. Are you able to move on from old relationships in a healthy manner?
3. Is your history free from hurt and pain caused by an abusive family, friend, or partner?
4. Have you never felt like one or both of your parents or other guardians abandoned you?
5. Do you have a loving relationship with your father and mother?
6. Was your household loving and nurturing while you were growing up?

If you have answered "yes" to the above questions and "no" to the questions about ungodly ties, you should give thanks to God for such a life. Perhaps God will use you to help set an example of healthy relationships for future generations. As you read through the rest of this book, think of how you might use it as a manual of healing for others.

On the other hand, if you did not grow up in a healthy, functioning home, be encouraged. This book is designed to help you overcome ungodly soul ties. *"He who has an ear, let him hear what the Spirit says to the churches. To him who overcomes I will give to eat from the tree of life, which is in the midst of the Paradise of God"* (Revelation 2:7).

Tomorrow, we are going to do something different. We are going to set aside self-examination for a bit and do some God-examination. Jesus said, *"This is eternal life, that they may know You, the only true God, and Jesus Christ whom You have sent"* (John 17:3). By studying God and His plan for the world, we can learn how to live life to its fullest, especially in our relationships.

HOMEWORK

Answer the following questions:

1. What did this self-evaluation help reveal to you?

2. What good things in your life should you hold on to?

3. Are there any evil things you need to let go of? Why?

4. According to Revelation 2:7, what do you get if you are an overcomer?

5. How would your life be different if you could overcome your negative soul ties?

6. Pray the prayers on the following page.

PRAYERS

1. Father, I am an overcomer.
2. Help me overcome, in Jesus' name.
3. Teach me to test all things, hold on to the good, and reject all evil.
4. Thank You for godly soul ties.
5. Remove all ungodly soul ties and replace them with godly ones.
6. Thank You for caring about my life, my relationships, and my soul.
7. Heal me from all hurt, pain, and abuse from my family, friends, and acquaintances.
8. I want to live whole, Lord.
9. Make me to be all that I can be in Christ Jesus.
10. I will eat of the Tree of Life in the Paradise of God, in Jesus' name.

DAY SIXTEEN

THE COSMIC BATTLE

And I will put enmity Between you and the woman, And between your seed and her Seed. He shall bruise your head, And you shall bruise His heel.

GENESIS 3:15

As Christians, we are in a cosmic battle against evil forces that seek to keep us in bondage to ungodly soul ties. *"For we do not wrestle against flesh and blood, but against principalities, against powers, against the rulers of the darkness of this age, against spiritual hosts of wickedness in the heavenly places"* (Ephesians 6:12). The battle for our souls began a long time ago in the Garden of Eden. From then on, the seed of the serpent has raged against the Seed of the woman, trying to destroy all things good.

Genesis 3:15 declares the gospel message in kernel form, revealing the victor of the battle as Jesus Christ. Today we will trace the Seed of Christ through the pages of Scripture. We'll see how God promises great blessing and power to us through Christ. Tomorrow we'll see what happens when Christ is born. And the next day, we'll discuss the great enemy of God, the seed of the serpent (Satan), and how God bruised his head, while bruising His own heel — declaring victory.

The Seed of the Woman

Through faith, the Seed of the woman (Christ) delivers all people from the schemes of Satan. In the NKJV, "Seed" is capitalized to acknowledge that the promised Seed is Christ. Recording the lineage of Christ (the Seed) is a major theme in the Bible. It begins in Genesis with Eve, who was looking forward to the One that would deliver mankind from the trickery of Satan. Each time Eve bore a son, she thought the child might be the promised Christ. However, God's plans would take thousands of years and many generations to manifest until a virgin would be with child.

Since death entered the world through Adam, the sinful nature was passed down through his offspring. *"For as in Adam all die, even so in Christ all shall be made alive"* (1 Corinthians 15:22). Christ had to be born of a (virgin) woman so the sinful nature would not be transferred covenantally through Adam. The offspring (Seed) of the virgin (Christ) would not carry the sinful nature of man because God (not man) would be the Child's Father.

Yet, until the time of Messiah, one of Eve's sons would have to carry on the line of the Seed. God chose Seth. He begat children, who also begat children until Noah was born. Through Noah came Shem, who would carry on the line until Abraham was born. God promised Abraham many blessings.

The Blessings of Abraham

Did you know that you can partake in all the blessings promised to Abraham? God revealed to Abraham in a unique way that he too would carry the Seed of the Messiah. He promised Abraham great blessings, saying: *"In your seed all the nations of the earth shall be blessed, because you have obeyed My voice"* (Genesis 22:18). Galatians 3:16 tells us that this seed is Christ: *"Now to Abraham and his Seed were the promises made. He does not say, 'And to seeds,' as of many, but as of one, 'And to your Seed,' who is Christ."*

The New Testament extends the promise to the entire Cosmos. *"For the promise that he would be the heir of the world [kosmos] was not to Abraham or to his seed through the law, but through the righteousness of faith"* (Romans 4:13). In Christ, you too are an heir of all the promises of Abraham. God promises: *"I will bless those who bless you, And I will curse him who curses you; And in you all the families of the earth shall be blessed"* (Genesis 12:3).

These promises are fulfilled the moment you believe the good news of Jesus Christ. Let's continue tracing the Seed through history. Genealogy matters.

The Eternal Throne of David

The accounts of Abraham, Isaac, and Jacob are well-known. But the Bible contains many other interesting (and even scandalous) stories of the lineage of Christ, including incest, adultery, and murder. Messiah (Jesus) came from the tribe of Judah, through incest between Judah and his daughter-in-law Tamar. Rahab was a harlot. Yet she was the mother of Boaz. The Bible tells the story of how Boaz met and married Ruth, a Moabitess. Ruth's baby, Obed, was the great grandfather of David, who would become king and carry the promised Seed of the Messiah.

Why would the Bible tell these stories? Because they show that God cares about outcasts, sinners, and broken people. Both tragedy and sin are part of Christ's lineage. He loves to use broken people for amazing purposes. If He can use these broken lives, He can use you too, despite your past soul ties and toxic relationships. But it gets better.

God promised David that his throne would be established forever. *"I will set up your seed after you...and I will establish the throne of his kingdom forever"* (2 Samuel 7:12-13). How is an eternal kingdom even possible? Christ would be the King who would ultimately rule on David's throne. Initially, the promise pointed to David's biological son Solomon, but ultimately it pointed to Christ. *"Has not the Scripture said that the Christ comes from the seed of David?"* (John 7:42).

After David, the line of Messiah split into two parts: Nathan carried the Seed of the woman through Mary; and Solomon carried the seed of Joseph (the supposed father of Jesus). We'll talk more about that tomorrow. If God uses broken people to bring about His good purposes in history, imagine what He can do for you.

HOMEWORK

Answer the following questions:

1. Who are the main players in the Cosmic Battle?

2. What is the gospel in kernel form?

3. Why did Jesus need to be born of a woman?

4. What did God promise Abraham? How do you partake of the promise?

5. How did God use broken people in His plan for redemption? What can He do for you?

6. Pray the prayers on the following page.

PRAYERS

1. Thank You, Father, for using broken people to accomplish Your perfect promises.
2. I surrender myself to You, Lord. Use me as You wish for Your good purposes.
3. Lord, thank You for giving me the victory over sin, self, and Satan.
4. Father, You are a promise keeper. Thank You for promising a Seed to rescue me.
5. I reject my association with Adam and choose Christ as my representative for life.
6. Forgive me for not trusting Your power more. Increase my faith.
7. Lord, I accept all the blessings of Abraham through Christ.
8. Thank You for supplying me an entrance into Your eternal Kingdom.
9. Your ways, O God, are far above my ways. Open my eyes.
10. Deliver me from the evil one. Heal all my brokenness, in Jesus' name. Amen!

DAY SEVENTEEN

BORN OF A VIRGIN

*And behold, you will conceive in your womb and bring
forth a Son, and shall call His name Jesus.*
Luke 1:31

Do you struggle with sin, self-confidence, or identity issues? If you do, you are not alone. Many people struggle to live life in the fullness of God's design, especially in relationships. Today, we are going to look at an aspect of Christ's birth that provides great hope over the power of sin and ungodly soul ties. Let's dive back into the genealogy of Jesus to see why.

God With Us

Legally, Jesus was the son of Joseph tracing back to Solomon. Physically, He was the son of God by the virgin Mary tracing to Nathan. Matthew records the genealogy of Jesus through Joseph. And Luke records the genealogy of Jesus through Mary. While both accounts are important, it is most significant that Mary was a virgin when she conceived Jesus by the power of the Holy Ghost. *"Behold, the virgin shall be with child, and bear a Son, and they shall call His name Immanuel," which is translated, 'God with us'"* (Matthew 1:23).

Jesus, by nature, is God through conception and human through the seed of the woman: God with us. This means Christ did not inherit the sinful nature of Adam. Rather, He had the sinless nature of God. This is good news for broken sinners.

The God-Man

No one can relate to sin, temptation, and sorrow better than our God. Jesus had a real body of flesh from Mary so He could be tempted like us in every way (Hebrews 4:15). This should provide great comfort to you. Why? Jesus knows what you are going through. Jesus understands your pain: He was tortured, despised, and rejected unto death. Jesus even took all of your iniquity upon Himself on the cross. Yet, He was without sin.

Since Jesus was also God in the flesh, He was able to resist the temptation to sin. And He resisted perfectly, which meant the grave could not hold Him. After His resurrection, Jesus ascended into heaven to sit at the right hand of God (on the throne of David) as the angel promised Mary: *"Do not be afraid, Mary...behold, you will conceive in your womb and bring forth a Son... and the Lord God will give Him the throne of His father David. And He will reign over the house of Jacob forever, and of His kingdom there will be no end"* (Luke 1:30-33). His Kingdom is forever. And, through faith, we inherit resurrection power to resist sin and see victory over Satan on earth as it is in heaven. Consider the promise of Isaiah 9:6-7:

> For unto us a Child is born,
> Unto us a Son is given;
> And the government will be upon His shoulder.
> And His name will be called
> Wonderful, Counselor, Mighty God,
> Everlasting Father, Prince of Peace.
>
> Of the increase of *His* government and peace
> There will be no end,
> Upon the throne of David and over His kingdom,
> To order it and establish it with judgment and justice
> From that time forward, even forever.
> The zeal of the Lord of hosts will perform this.

Christ's kingdom would start at His birth and only increase in justice, righteousness, and peace on the throne of David until forever. And it would be the zeal of the Lord of hosts that would accomplish it. We have access to all this through faith. Do you believe it?

Thy Kingdom Came

You, beloved, are a partaker in Christ's everlasting Kingdom. Ever since the promise of the Seed in Genesis 3:15, Israel was looking for her coming Messiah. And when He arrived, the first thing Jesus preached was, *"Repent, for the kingdom of heaven is at hand"* (Matthew 4:17).

Sadly, *"He came to His own, and His own did not receive Him. But as many as received Him, to them He gave the right to become children of God, to those who believe in His name"* (John 1:11-12). While Christ's own people rejected Him, His death, resurrection, and exaltation made it possible for all men and nations to become God's chosen people through faith.

Children of Promise

In Christ, we are no longer children of Adam. Instead, we are the children of God through faith. Everyone who believes in Christ partakes in all the blessings of Abraham. *"And if you are Christ's, then you are Abraham's seed, and heirs according to the promise"* (Galatians 3:29).

Plus, through faith, we are partakers in the everlasting Kingdom promised to David's seed. *"Therefore, brethren, be even more diligent to make your call and election sure, for if you do these things you will never stumble; for so an entrance will be supplied to you abundantly into the everlasting kingdom of our Lord and Savior Jesus Christ"* (2 Peter 1:10-11).

Now, we must live according to these truths. Let's break free from the negative influences of ungodly soul ties and live in the reality of the blessings of Abraham. Let us also take advantage of all the promises of God because we are part of His eternal Kingdom. Satan has no power over us.

Prayer of Victory

When we pray as Christ taught His disciples, *"Your kingdom come. Your will be done on earth as it is in heaven,"* we are asking God to bring more of heaven (His Kingdom) down to earth. Godly men and scholars of the past have explained that when we pray for His Kingdom to come, we are petitioning God to:[2]

1. Govern us by His Word and Spirit so that we might submit to Him more and more;
2. Preserve and increase His Church;
3. Destroy the works of the devil;
4. Smash every power that exalts itself against God;
5. Demolish all wicked devices formed against His Holy Word; and to
6. Do so until the fullness of His Kingdom comes;
7. Wherein He shall be all in all. Amen.

---

[2] Adapted from the Heidelberg Catechism Question 123: What is the second petition (in the Lord's Prayer)?

Praying according to Christ's command is petitioning God to grant victory to Christ's church. If God asked us to pray for it, do you believe He will grant it? *"And I also say to you…on this rock I will build My church, and the gates of Hades shall not prevail against it"* (Matthew 16:18).

Christ will prevail in history, and He can prevail in your life over all sin and Satanic powers if you will seek Him. God promised it from the beginning. We'll look more at how Christ conquered the enemy (the seed of the serpent) tomorrow. Today, believe in faith that you also have the victory.

HOMEWORK

Answer the following questions:

1. Why do Matthew and Luke record different genealogies of Jesus?

2. What is significant about the virgin birth?

3. How can Jesus relate to your suffering, pain, and struggles with sin?

4. What did Jesus first preach?

5. What is the significance of praying the Lord's prayer?

6. Pray the prayers on the following page.

PRAYERS

1. Lord, thank You for understanding my weaknesses.
2. Father, thank You for sending Your Son, Jesus to be God with us.
3. I want to see Your Kingdom come more and more on earth and in my life.
4. Increase my faith to know and understand Your great power toward me.
5. Lord, bring Your justice, righteousness, and peace to earth as it is in heaven.
6. Thank You for establishing an eternal kingdom and allowing me to partake of it.
7. Govern me by Your Word and Spirit so that I might submit to You more and more.
8. Preserve and increase my influence in the world so I can help build Your Church.
9. Destroy the works of the devil in my life, home, family, and world.
10. Smash every power that exalts itself against God, and demolish all wicked devices formed against Your holy Word. Amen!

DAY EIGHTEEN

THE DEATH BLOW

*For this purpose the Son of God was manifested, that
He might destroy the works of the devil.*
1 John 3:8

Do you ever get fed up with how sin destroys your relationships? You might be tired of struggling with your own pride, lusts, or bitterness. Perhaps your heart aches over the sin that is destroying a loved one caught up in addiction, pornography, or sexual immorality. You might even weep over the sins of the nation like abortion, perversion, and hatred toward God.

No one hates sin more than God. The entire trajectory of history has been to redeem people from sin's clutch. This is the very reason Jesus was born. Over the last couple of days, we've looked at the Seed of the woman: Christ. Today, we will look deeper into the seed of the serpent, namely Satan. In Genesis 3:15, God promised to put enmity between the seed of the serpent and the Seed of the woman. This enmity is the battle cry of Scripture. But God promised to deliver a fatal blow to Satan. And He did.

The Offspring of Satan

All men (and women) are born in sin and therefore subject to Satan and his devices. You could say that without Christ, all men are the seed (or offspring) of Satan because of sin. *"He who sins is of the devil, for the devil has sinned from the beginning* (1 John 3:8). The seed of Satan includes all sin and all things that are under the sway of sin.

Thankfully, that is not the end of the story, nor the conclusion of 1 John 3:8: *"For this purpose the Son of God was manifested, that He might destroy the works of the devil."* We'll talk more about Christ's victory over Satan in a bit. First, let's trace the seed of the Serpent by again looking at the historical narratives in the Bible.

The Seed of the Serpent

We don't have to read far into the book of Genesis to see the effects of the curse on the human race. Almost immediately, Satan rears his ugly head to snuff out the righteous seed that might bear the promised Messiah. Let's trace some key characters and events in the Cosmic Battle that lead up to Christ's death.

- **Cain and Abel:** Sinful Cain killed his righteous brother Abel. Cain went out from the presence of the Lord and his offspring continued in sin, with Lamech following in his murderous ways. Lamech also became the first polygamist. The seed of Satan continued to corrupt the earth through intermarriage until every intent of the thoughts of man's heart was only evil continually (Genesis 6:5). The only hope to preserve the righteous seed was for God to intervene.
- **The Flood:** The Lord's solution was to destroy the wicked seed of Satan from the earth in a flood. One man, Noah, found favor in the eyes of God. The Lord instructed Noah to build an ark to preserve him and his family alive. But that did not stop Satan from planting his seed in Noah's son Ham, the father of the Canaanites and the father of Nimrod.
- **Tower of Babel:** God commanded Noah's family to multiply and fill the earth, but sin again had corrupted the earth. The people rebelled against God and settled instead in the land of Shinar. Rather than spreading out as God commanded, they built a tower to the heavens. The Bible records that they would have been successful in their sin and rebellion without intervention. So God confused their language, forcing them to scatter abroad and fill the earth.
- **Blood Battles:** Throughout history, enmity continued between the two seeds. Ishmael and Isaac were both sons of Abraham. One came through faith and the other through sin. Jacob and Esau battled inside the womb. Yet, Jacob God loved and Esau He hated. David and Saul were both anointed by God as king, yet Saul sought to kill David who was a man after God's own heart. The battle between the seeds continued until the virgin was with Child.
- **Attempts Against Messiah:** When the Seed of the woman was finally born, Satan's efforts ramped up. Satan tried to kill Christ many times. First, he incited Herod to slaughter all the babies in an attempt to destroy the newborn King. Later, Satan tempted Jesus to jump off the pinnacle of the Temple. With hearts fueled by jealousy, the Jewish leaders sought to kill Jesus. His own friend, Judas, betrayed Him to death. Eventually, the seed of the serpent

was successful in killing the Messiah. Satan thought he had won the Cosmic Battle when the Romans crucified Jesus on a cross.

As Christ uttered His last words on the cross, "It is finished," Satan thought he had finally destroyed the Seed of the woman. What he didn't know, was that he had signed his own death warrant.

The Fatal Blow

Christ's birth and life were the beginning of Satan's defeat. It was the reason He was born. *"For this purpose the Son of God was manifested, that He might destroy the works of the devil"* (1 John 3:8). Christ came to deliver a fatal blow to Satan. While on earth, Christ demonstrated this by healing the sick, casting out demons, and setting straight the misunderstandings of His Law.

Then, Jesus offered Himself as a sacrifice for our sins so that He might accomplish the victory for us. When He died on the cross, the Seed of the woman stomped on the head of the serpent. Yes, Jesus was bruised, beaten, and crucified (*you shall bruise His heel*). But He would recover in three days. Satan, on the other hand, received a head wound unto death (*He shall bruise your head*). The Bible records that Christ's death would do the following magnificent feats:

1. **Deliver** us from Satan's power in this evil age (Galatians 1:4).
2. **Destroy** Satan (Hebrews 2:14).
3. **Release** us from Satan's bondage (Hebrews 2:15).
4. **Remove** the fear of death (Hebrews 2:15).
5. **Rescue** us from Satan's domain and transfer us into the eternal Kingdom (Colossians 1:13).
6. **Redeem** us from every lawless deed (Titus 2:14).
7. **Purify** us from evil so we can be God's own possession (Titus 2:14).
8. **Cast out** the devil from the world (John 12:31).
9. **Remove** Satan's access to heaven (Luke 10:18).
10. **Proclaim** judgment on the devil (John 16:11).
11. **Disarm** Satan's power (Colossians 2:15).
12. **Reveal** that Christ had triumphed over Satan (Colossians 2:15).
13. **Crush** Satan under our feet (Romans 16:20).
14. **Overcome** the evil one (1 John 2:14).
15. **Grant** us the power to cast out demons (Mark 16:17).

Christ's death on the cross removed Satan's legal authority to bind men under sin and death because of Adam's sin. It was the fatal blow that was Satan's undoing. We can partake in the victory when we stand in the authority of Christ.

Satan and his demons are still on earth seeking people to devour and destroy. However, the fatal wound will cause the devil's influence in the world to decrease over time as people submit themselves to the Lordship of Jesus Christ. This is our victory in Christ. "*These things I have spoken to you, that in Me you may have peace. In the world you will have tribulation; but be of good cheer, I have overcome the world*" (John 16:33).

Christ has overcome the world, the flesh, and the devil. Will you live in His power? He can heal you, restore your relationships, destroy all your Satanic soul ties, and bring about the abundant life Christ promised. Jesus wants to take back everything the devil stole from you and give you life instead. "*The thief does not come except to steal, and to kill, and to destroy. I have come that they may have life, and that they may have it more abundantly*" (John 10:10).

Now that you have your marching orders and know your victory in Christ, we are going to start taking more ground from the devil by examining the doorways he uses to hold you in bondage. To thrive in all your relationships, you must first do some housecleaning. Get ready for battle, beloved of God!

HOMEWORK

Answer the following questions:

1. Why did Jesus come into this world?

2. Who are the offspring of Satan?

3. How has Satan tried to destroy the Seed of the woman through history?

4. What was Satan's fatal mistake?

5. What is the outcome of Christ's death? And how does it affect you personally?

6. Pray the prayers on the following page.

PRAYERS

1. Lord, thank You for coming to destroy the works of the devil.
2. Father, please destroy the works of the devil in my life.
3. I hate sin and sin's effect on my life. I reject Satan's attempts to destroy me.
4. Lord, I want nothing to do with the seed of the serpent and his evil plans.
5. I accept the death of Jesus on my behalf to destroy the works of the devil.
6. Deliver me from Satan's power and release me from all bondages and ungodly soul ties.
7. Remove me from Satan's domain and transfer me into the Kingdom of Christ.
8. Heal me, restore my relationships, destroy all my Satanic soul ties, and bring about the abundant life Christ promised.
9. Lord, You have overcome the world. Grant me the power to overcome sin, self, and Satan.
10. Jesus, please restore everything the devil has stolen from me and grant me Your abundant life instead.

DAY NINETEEN

SILVER CORD PORTALS

Remember your Creator before the silver cord is loosed, Or the golden bowl is broken, Or the pitcher shattered at the fountain, Or the wheel broken at the well.

ECCLESIASTES 12:6

If you still do not believe we are in a war against Satan and his demons, consider this true story as related in a sermon titled *Irrational Paranoia, Jealousy, Anger, & Hatred* by Dr. Phillip Kayser:

> A pastor named Steve was traveling by airplane when he noticed that the man sitting two seats over was thumbing through some little cards and moving his lips.
>
> The man looked professorial with his goatee and graying brown hair, and Steve placed him at fifty-something. Guessing the man was a fellow-believer, Steve leaned over to engage him in conversation.
>
> "Looks to me like you're memorizing something," he said.
>
> "No, actually I was praying," the man said.
>
> Steve introduced himself. "I believe in prayer too," he said.
>
> "Well, I have a specific assignment," said the man with the goatee.
>
> "What's that?" Steve asked.
>
> "I'm praying for the downfall of Christian pastors."
>
> "I would certainly fit into that category," Steve said. "Is my name on the list?"
>
> "Not on *my* list," the man replied.[3]

If we are not warring against the demonic realm as we ought, we can be certain that they are warring against us. One of the weapons that Satan uses against Christians is ungodly silver cords, which attempt to create soul ties by summoning demons through prayer, rituals, or curses.

---

[3] https://kaysercommentary.com/Sermons/LifeOfDavid/1Samuel%2018_8-16.md#fnref2

What Are Silver Cords?

Silver cords could be described as the life thread that attaches our spirit to our body. When we die, the silver cord is broken and our spirit returns to God while our bodies return to the dust until the resurrection. You can think of a silver cord as a type of umbilical cord similar to the one that connects a fetus to its mother. The silver cord transmits life and spiritual energy to the body.

Solomon talks about the loosing of the silver cord in Ecclesiastes 12:6-7: *"Remember your Creator before the silver cord is loosed, Or the golden bowl is broken, Or the pitcher shattered at the fountain, Or the wheel broken at the well. Then the dust will return to the earth as it was, And the spirit will return to God who gave it."* He is referring to death.

While the silver cord mentioned in Ecclesiastes is designed by God, Satan seeks ways to use the concept for evil, creating ungodly silver cords. Without delving too deeply into the things of Satan, which is strictly forbidden (see Revelation 2:20-24), we will try to give a simple explanation of how Satan corrupts these silver cords.

Unholy people such as Satanists, witches, sorcerers, warlocks, and wizards may seek to use the silver cord God has given them to travel outside their bodies through occult practices. Just as the man in the story above was "assigned" to pray for the downfall of pastors, these wicked people seek to "visit" their victims in the spirit realm for nefarious purposes.

If a Christian is a target of such an attack, and they are not protected due to ignorance, sin, or an ungodly soul tie, the human spirit can do harm to the targeted individual.

Armor of God

Christians ought not to be unaware of the schemes of the devil. Nor, should they live in fear. Instead, Christians must take up the armor of God to fight against him in the power of the Spirit.

Let's review your armor and your call to arms in Ephesians 6:10-18.

- **Be strong** in the Lord and in His mighty power (Ephesians 6:10).
- **Put on** the whole armor of God so you may stand against the wiles of the devil (Ephesians 6:11).
- **Do** everything to withstand the evil in the day you are visited (Ephesians 6:13).
- **Gird** your waist with truth, which is the Word of God (Ephesians 6:14).
- **Wear** the twofold breastplate of righteousness, which is found in Christ's righteousness and holy conduct (Ephesians 6:14).

- **Shod your feet** with the gospel of shalom, which includes peace with God through salvation and peace with man through holiness (Ephesians 6:15).
- **Take up** the shield of faith (believe God's promises) which will quench all the fiery darts of the wicked one (Ephesians 6:16).
- **Wield** the sword of the Spirit by speaking God's promises (Ephesians 6:17).
- **Put on** the helmet of salvation, which will allow nothing to harm you without God's permission (Ephesians 6:17).
- **Pray always** in the Spirit, i.e., according to the Word of God (Ephesians 6:18).
- **Be watchful** for the schemes of the devil (Ephesians 6:18).
- **Persevere** and do not stop fighting against Satan's schemes (Ephesians 6:18).

You might wonder how you can know if a "silver cord" attack comes against you. The first thing to remember is that God will be a hedge to you if you are walking in righteousness, abiding in Christ, and confessing and forsaking sin. However, if you wake up with an irrational and overwhelming fear, sense a presence in your room, hear voices in your head, see flashes of light or hallucinations that you cannot explain, you might have an open doorway to an ungodly silver cord through unconfessed sin or an ungodly soul tie.

Your immediate response should be to call upon the name of Jesus Christ to protect you. Speak His name out loud if you can. Ask Him to cut the ungodly cord and reveal to you any sin in your life that might allow the attack. If He brings something to mind, confess it. Plead the blood of Jesus until the demonic intruder leaves. Ask God to seal up any portals or doorways that would allow the visitor to return. God is more powerful than any demonic attack, directed curse, satanic prayer, or ungodly silver cord sent your way.

HOMEWORK

Answer the following questions:

1. What is the difference between a godly silver cord and an ungodly silver cord?

2. What are the weapons of warfare you can use against an ungodly silver cord?

3. If you could speak only one word to battle Satan, what would it be?

4. What might open you up to an attack by an ungodly silver cord?

5. Spend time meditating upon the full armor of God so that you can stand against the wiles of the devil. See Ephesians 6:10-18.

6. Pray the prayers on the following page.

PRAYERS

1. Father, I thank You for Your mighty power against all the schemes of Satan.
2. Help me daily take up the full armor of God to stand firm against Satan's schemes.
3. Protect me and my family from every attempt of Satan to visit me with a demonic silver cord.
4. Hedge me about so that no scheme of Satan will prosper against me or my family.
5. I plead the blood of Jesus on my life and the life of my family against all demonic attempts to visit me for harm.
6. I confess and forsake the sins of pride, false humility, rebellion, and any other sin that might give Satan ground in my life.
7. Break every scheme of Satan, witches, wizards, warlocks, and demons to create a soul tie with me.
8. Remove anything and everything that might link or connect me to the demonic realm.
9. Station Your mighty warrior angels to protect me and my family from ungodly silver cords.
10. Break every evil prayer chain, power, or network of spiritual wickedness against me or my family, in the name of Jesus Christ.

DAY TWENTY

ACCURSED OBJECTS

And you, by all means abstain from the accursed things, lest you become accursed when you take of the accursed things, and make the camp of Israel a curse, and trouble it.

Joshua 6:18

After the death of his alcoholic brother, a Christian man was entrusted with liquidating his brother's estate. The brother was a godless man, who rejected Christ openly. Many of his possessions were given away, thrown out, or sold. However, the surviving brother saw some sharp-looking shirts hanging in the closet and decided to keep them for himself.

While there was nothing sinful in taking the clothes for himself, the brother began to notice strange things while wearing the shirts. He felt lustful urges, had unclean feelings, and saw certain things in the physical realm that were not working according to the normal laws of nature. The brother "sensed" that demons were somehow attached to the garments and choose to discard them immediately. At that time, the unusual manifestations ceased.

Forbidden Items in the Bible

Many Christians falsely believe that demons cannot "possess" or attach themselves to physical items. However, there is ample evidence to the contrary in Scripture. The most persuasive passage comes from the Old Testament, where God prohibited the children of Israel from taking the accursed things from Jericho (see the quote at beginning of the chapter). It is not clear if the items were accursed because God forbid them or if God forbid them because they were accursed. Likely, it was both.

Jericho and other nations that Israel was commanded to dispossess, were wicked, godless nations who practiced all kinds of abominations, witchcraft, and idolatry. God warned that if the children of Israel took the "accursed" items from Jericho, that the camp of Israel would become a curse and the items would bring trouble.

The New Testament also warns about touching "unclean" things and ties these unclean things to idols (2 Corinthians 6:14-18) and demons (Acts 8:7). In fact, when people sacrifice to idols, they are actually sacrificing to demons. *"What am I saying then? That an idol is anything, or what is offered to idols is anything? Rather, that the things which the Gentiles sacrifice they sacrifice to demons and not to God, and I do not want you to have fellowship with demons"* (1 Corinthians 10:19-20). God does not want us to have fellowship (or a soul tie) with demons.

Soul Ties with Stuff

We must guard against having an ungodly soul tie with stuff through the spiritual realm. If we allow accursed things into our life, it can bring the same kinds of cursing and hardship God warned about in Joshua 6:18, creating a fellowship with demons that can bring us great harm. Let's look at several categories of items that can create a soul tie.

1. **Occult Items:** Any item that is used in witchcraft, astrology, sorcery, Wiccan, demon-worship, satanism, magic, voodoo, fortune-telling, astral-projection, mind-reading, necromancy, seances, or any other occult practice is subject to demonic attachment.

    Items might include tarot cards, ouija boards, astrology charts, zodiac signs, fortune cookies, voodoo dolls, magic books, magic wands, incantations, ritual clothing, crystal balls, ingredients for spells, satanic bibles, palm-reading charts, fetishes, charms, lucky rabbit's feet, potions, or any other item associated in any way with any occult practice. If you have such things, burn them (no matter the value) as they did in the early church (Acts 19:19). You do not want to pass these demonically charged items along to others.

2. **Idols and Things Sacrificed to Idols:** God forbids us to have anything to do with idols and things sacrificed to idols. In America, our idols are not as openly manifested as in other countries. Nevertheless, idolatry is alive and well and we are commanded to flee from it. Anything that we love more than God can be an idol. Some top examples include self, social media, technology, fame, money, material wealth, sports, celebrities, etc. Any one of these things can cause a demonic soul tie in your life.

    However, there are still "household" idols in America, including statues of Buddha, Shiva, Brahma, Krishna, Vishnu, Moloch, Baphomet, crucifixes, prayer beads, totem poles, images of Mary, etc. Even Christian paraphernalia can become idols if worshipped or improperly adored, such as crosses and images of Christ. Plus, you must beware when eating at restaurants that display idols, as the food may be dedicated to demons.

3. **Accursed Gifts:** People involved in satanism or the occult can pronounce curses on items and gift them to people in an effort to gain a foothold or soul tie in their life. You must be careful when receiving a gift from someone you do not know or someone you know is involved in occultism or any form of demon worship.

4. **Items of False Religions:** All wisdom that is not from God is demonic. That means false religions are powered by demons. Stay away from all items, books, and material from cults and religions other than true Christianity.

5. **Pornography:** If you have pornographic material in your home, it is opening your life up to demonic attack. Destroy it immediately.

6. **Drug Paraphernalia:** Whether legal or illegal, drugs are driven on by demonic forces. If you have any drugs in your home or paraphernalia to use the drug, you are opening your home to demons. This applies to some prescription drugs as well, as many of them are tested on or made from aborted babies. Do everything in your power to get off prescription drugs if able.

7. **Wicked Possessions:** Any object that once belonged to someone steeped in deep sin or wickedness could carry demons with it. You don't want to live in fear of every object you own. However, if you "sense" that something "feels" unclean, take every precaution and discard the item.

This list cannot possibly cover every possible danger. However, it should be enough to get you started with a good house cleaning. If you have any of these objects in your home, throw them out or destroy them as soon as possible. The final step is to break the demonic soul tie through prayer.

HOMEWORK

Answer the following questions:

1. What is the biblical foundation for soul ties with objects?

2. Why doesn't God want you to have fellowship with demons?

3. Take inventory of your belongings. Which items are potential invitations to demons? Remove them.

4. Research all your prescription medications to evaluate if they were made with or tested on aborted fetal tissue.

5. If you are struggling to destroy any accursed thing, remember that there is a demon behind it.

6. Pray the prayers on the following page.

PRAYERS

1. Father, search my heart and my house. Reveal any accursed thing that might leave room for Satan to harm me and my family.
2. Cleanse my heart and home of every accursed thing.
3. I plead the blood of Christ and renounce all soul ties with demons in my home and heart.
4. Let me love nothing more than I love You, Jesus.
5. I offer all my belongings to You, Lord. Remove every accursed thing.
6. Take all my idols of self, pride, possessions, and passions. Destroy them, Lord.
7. Lord, I renounce all connections with the occult, idols, accursed gifts, false religions, pornography, and drugs.
8. Remove anything and everything in my home that might open a door in my life to the demonic realm.
9. Send Your mighty warrior angels to bind and remove all legal ground Satan has in my life through accursed things.
10. I surrender everything in my heart and home to you, Lord, in the name of Jesus Christ.

DAY TWENTY-ONE

BLOOD COVENANTS

So they cried aloud, and cut themselves, as was their custom, with knives and lances, until the blood gushed out on them.

1 KINGS 18:28

Blood is sacred. It contains the very life force of humans and animals. This is why God forbids the eating or drinking of blood. Plus, blood is the substance God chose to make "atonement" for sin. *"For the life of the flesh is in the blood, and I have given it to you upon the altar to make atonement for your souls; for it is the blood that makes atonement for the soul"* (Leviticus 17:11). Blood plays a significant role in the history of mankind.

The Dividing Line

Just as the Bible is divided into two parts (Old Testament and New Testament), history can also be divided by two covenants: the Old Covenant and the New Covenant. In fact, the words testament and covenant can be used interchangeably (see Hebrews 9:16-22). Plus, where the Old Testament intersects with the New Testament, the line of history divides. BC marks the time before Christ's birth (Old Testament) and AD (anno domini — or the year of our Lord) marks the time after Christ's birth (New Testament). We could rightfully, then, call the two books of the Bible the Old Covenant and the New Covenant.

Both the Old and New Covenants were ratified with blood. Moses inaugurated the Old Covenant with the blood of animals: *"For when Moses had spoken every precept to all the people according to the law, he took the blood of calves and goats, with water, scarlet wool, and hyssop, and sprinkled both the book itself and all the people, saying, 'This is the blood of the covenant which God has commanded you'"* (Hebrews 9:19-20). Jesus inaugurated the New Covenant with His own blood, putting an end to animal sacrifice once for all time.

What Are Covenants?

Covenants are agreements between two people or parties. In ancient times, covenants consisted of various parts, including the names of the parties, oaths to obey, promised blessings for obedience, and curses or consequences for disobedience. These covenants were often ratified by the shedding of blood. Many Bible scholars have noted that the Old and New Covenants in the Bible are structured according to these ancient covenants.

For example, Yahweh God, set forth the stipulations for the nation of Israel to obey a set of laws. If they obeyed, God promised blessings. If they disobeyed, God promised curses. Israel joined in a covenant with God to obey everything He commanded and ratified the agreement with blood. *"Then he took the Book of the Covenant and read in the hearing of the people. And they said, 'All that the Lord has said we will do, and be obedient.' And Moses took the blood, sprinkled it on the people, and said, 'This is the blood of the covenant which the Lord has made with you according to all these words'"* (Exodus 24:7-8).

When we become a Christian, we also enter into a "blood covenant" with Christ. We enter into the covenant by an oath of baptism through the shed blood of Jesus Christ, who instructs us to *"observe all things that I have commanded you"* (Matthew 28:20). This is all spelled out in the great commission, though many people neglect to see the covenantal nature of salvation and the necessary obedience. The Old Covenant was the law written on tablets of stone. The New Covenant is the law written on our hearts (Jeremiah 31:31-33). Both covenants were initiated with blood.

Counterfeit Covenants

Satan understands the significance of blood in ratifying covenants, and, in his usual fashion, has a counterfeit. Many Satanic practices include blood sacrifices for this reason. The shedding of blood against the commandments of God increases Satan's power. This is why Christians must forgo anything that might create a counterfeit blood covenant, thereby creating an ungodly soul tie that opens them up to demonic influence. Beware of these potential counterfeit blood covenants, where blood might be shed in an unholy manner:

- **Cutting:** Harming your body through cutting is an unholy way to seek relief from pain and emotional scars. It is demonic and can open you up to further demonic control. Repent of and cease this practice in the name of Jesus.

- **Tattoos:** Marking your body is expressly forbidden in the Bible (Leviticus 19:28). Tattoos shed sacred blood and can open you up to the demonic influences of tattoo artists and other familiar spirits. Confess and forsake this practice, and ask God to break any ungodly soul ties that have resulted from the tattoo.
- **Fornication:** In the Bible, a virgin could defend her innocence against unfaithfulness by presenting a "cloth" to her accusing husband (Deuteronomy 22:17). Many believe this cloth would be stained with blood on the wedding night as proof of chastity. Marriage was "ratified" by a blood covenant through intercourse. Sexual relations outside of marriage "join" two people together in a soul tie ratified by blood. Abstain from all forms of sexual immorality.
- **Medicine:** Many pharmaceutical drugs are tested on and made with aborted babies. If you partake in such medicine unknowingly, you are opening yourself up to an unholy alliance through the shedding of innocent blood. Research any and all medicine to be sure they are not tainted with the sacrificed blood of babies. Many childhood and adult vaccines are especially tainted, containing the fetal DNA fragments from aborted babies. Also, it would be wise to seek the Lord diligently about taking a blood transfusion from someone you do not know. Store your own blood if possible for cases of emergency.
- **Eating Blood:** From the beginning, God has forbidden the eating of blood. Plus, this law is reiterated in the New Covenant. *"We write to them to abstain from things polluted by idols, from sexual immorality, from things strangled, and from blood"* (Acts 15:20). Reject any food or drink that uses blood as an ingredient.
- **Cannibalism:** Some cultures still engage in cannibalism. In western culture, it mostly exists in deranged and demonized people. However, there is a resurgence of cannibalism through modern medicine. For example, the oral Adenovirus vaccine was cultured on cells derived from an aborted baby. It is impossible to filter out the human remains. Other vaccines and medicines, like Enbrel, contain aborted human remains. Injecting or consuming accursed items can bring upon you harm we do not understand. Find out which products are suspect at Cogforlife.com.
- **Skin Care Products:** Several anti-aging skin creams contain fetal DNA fragments from aborted babies. You do not want to be rubbing the remains of murdered babies on your face as a Satanic fountain of youth. For more information, visit Cogforlife.com.
- **Food:** To our knowledge, there are no foods that contain fetal DNA from aborted babies. However, some companies use aborted fetal cell lines to test artificial flavors. Firmenich, Ajinomoto, and Nestles use Senomyx (a product made with aborted fetal cells) to test

artificial food flavors. We are called to have nothing to do with the unfruitful deeds of darkness. Boycott these companies. To learn what specific products to avoid, visit Cogforlife.com.
- **Drugs:** Injectable street drugs pose multiple risks. First, drug use can open you up to the spiritual realm in a negative way. Second, the needles draw blood, opening you up to soul ties with demons from the drug dealer, manufacturer, or anyone you are using drugs with. Third, if you use a dirty needle, you put yourself at further risk. Stay away from this dark enemy of your soul.

Be vigilant and stand against the schemes of the devil. Stay away from anything that might institute a blood covenant that opens you up to demonic soul ties. If you have opened yourself up to one or more of these things, James 4:7-10 provides the seven-fold solution to deliverance:

1. *Therefore submit to God.*
2. *Resist the devil and he will flee from you.*
3. *Draw near to God and He will draw near to you.*
4. *Cleanse your hands, you sinners; and purify your hearts, you double-minded.*
5. *Lament and mourn and weep!*
6. *Let your laughter be turned to mourning and your joy to gloom.*
7. *Humble yourselves in the sight of the Lord, and He will lift you up.*

HOMEWORK

Answer the following questions:

1. Why is blood sacred to God?

2. What divides the line of history?

3. What is similar about the Old and New Covenants? What is the major difference between the Old and New Covenants?

4. Did you take your oath to obey Jesus seriously when you were baptized?

5. Have you knowingly or unknowingly put yourself at risk of a counterfeit blood covenant? Confess and forsake them.

6. Pray the prayers on the following page.

PRAYERS

1. Father, thank you for taking me into Your bloodline through Jesus Christ.
2. Cleanse my heart, home, and family from every counterfeit blood covenant.
3. Apply the blood of Jesus Christ to all my known and unknown blood covenants not initiated by You.
4. I submit all things to You, Lord, in faith.
5. Give me the power to resist the devil and all his hateful temptations.
6. Help me draw near to You so that You will draw near to me. I need You to overcome.
7. Cleanse my hands and purify my heart with the true blood of the covenant poured out by Jesus Christ.
8. Cause me to weep and mourn over my sin, Lord.
9. Where there is sin, turn my laughter to mourning and my joy gloom.
10. I humble myself before You, Lord. Please, lift me up and deliver me from every false way, in Jesus' name.

DAY TWENTY-TWO:

UNHOLY AFFECTIONS

For this reason God gave them up to vile passions.
ROMANS 1:26

Just as with our first parents, sin commonly begins in the heart with a desire for some forbidden thing. Many men, including pastors, have fallen from grace by acting on these unholy affections. And, once given into: "Sin takes you farther than you want to go, keeps you longer than you want to stay, and costs you more than you want to pay." Sin can start with a simple glance and end up costing you your life. If we do not keep our flesh in check, God will give us over to vile passions, confirming us in our sin.

God Gave Them Up

These words, *"God gave them up,"* are words no one wants to hear. Yet, that is exactly what happens when a person exchanges the truth of God for a lie. Romans chapter one is a call to people who are engaged in unholy affections to sever the soul ties before it is too late.

How exactly does God give someone over to vile passions? It happens when God removes His gracious loving hand of protection and allows Satan to have free-reign in a person's life. If the person is a believer, we can hope and pray for God to use the "giving over" as a call to repentance.

Paul warns the Corinthian church how to handle people who are engaged in vile passions: *"Deliver such a one to Satan for the destruction of the flesh, that his spirit may be saved in the day of the Lord Jesus* (1 Corinthians 5:5).

If you are even flirting with unholy passions, you are opening a doorway to demons that will be powerfully hard, if not impossible, to shut. *"Each one is tempted when he is drawn away by his own desires and enticed. Then, when desire has conceived, it gives birth to sin; and sin, when it is full-grown, brings forth death"* (James 1:14-15).

Thou Shall Not Covet

What exactly is a vile passion or unholy affection? A quick look at the tenth commandment will provide a clue. "*You shall not covet your neighbor's house; you shall not covet your neighbor's wife, nor his male servant, nor his female servant, nor his ox, nor his donkey, nor anything that is your neighbor's*" (Exodus 20:17). An unholy passion can be desiring something that does not belong to you. But there is more.

Romans 1:24-25 informs us that God also gives people over to "*uncleanness, in the lusts of their hearts, to dishonor their bodies among themselves, who exchanged the truth of God for the lie, and worshiped and served the creature rather than the Creator, who is blessed forever. Amen.*"

A vile affection is any desiring or coveting something that belongs to a neighbor or is forbidden by God. The desire may start small, but if not stopped immediately, the lust for the thing grows and grows until we dwell upon it in our minds, and then act upon it. A small sinful desire can become a huge beastly sin that consumes us unto death. This can even happen to professing Christians. I Corinthians 11:30 warns that unconfessed sin can lead to sickness, weakness, and death: "*For this reason many are weak and sick among you, and many sleep* [i.e. are dead]." The solution is to examine our hearts, confess our sins, and forsake our shameful lusts.

Sinful Desires

There is a false movement in the Christian church claiming that ungodly desires are not sinful; They maintain it is only acting upon the sin that breaks covenant with God. Yet, that is not at all what Jesus taught, nor James, nor anyone in the Bible. Jesus said if we even look at someone with lust in our heart, we are guilty of adultery. "*But I say to you that whoever looks at a woman to lust for her has already committed adultery with her in his heart*" (Matthew 5:28). We must possess our vessels with honor, "*not in passion of lust, like the Gentiles who do not know God*" (1 Thessalonians 4:5).

Lust is a sin. We must cut off all coveting and sinful desires before they have a chance to bear the fruit of sin. Immediately upon having a sinful desire, you must confess and forsake it. If you allow your mind to linger for even a moment on an unholy affection, you are opening yourself up to a demonic soul tie that can lead to destruction.

Even legitimate affections can be turned to illegitimate if acted upon in an ungodly fashion. For example, sexual intimacy is to be enjoyed inside of lawful marriage. Outside, it breaks God's commandments. God gave wine to provide joy to the heart of man (Psalm 104:14), but drunkenness is a sin. Food is made to delight the senses and nourish the body, but gluttony is an offense sometimes worthy of death (Deuteronomy 21:20-21). In these cases, it takes wisdom from the Holy Spirit to know if you are crossing into dangerous territory. It is wise to err on caution.

Cautious Affections

Let's look closer at 10 affections that can lead to demonic soul ties. If you have any of these in your life, take note and deal with them promptly.

1. **Food:** We mentioned previously that food itself is a blessing from God. Yet, when you are tempted to overeat to the point of discomfort, eat for pleasure only, and have no self-control at the dinner table, you could open yourself up to a demonic soul tie that leads toward gluttony, sickness, and death.
2. **Alcohol:** While alcohol is a blessing from God, it can also be a curse. Drunkenness is a sin. If you cannot restrain yourself with alcohol, you are not an alcoholic. Rather, you have been given over to demonic passions, and the Bible calls you a drunkard. According to 1 Corinthians 6:10, drunkards will not inherit the kingdom of God. If you have an unholy affection for alcohol, turn from it today.
3. **Sex:** Sexual desire is normal and natural. It is part of what brings two people together in marriage. However, lusting for sex outside of marriage is a sin. This includes lusting after someone you PLAN to marry. The desire should be there for your future spouse, but you must not entertain it lest it bears the fruit of sin. Do nothing to incite or entice passions outside of marriage, including passionate kissing.
4. **OPT:** Other people's things (OPT) are off-limits. Do not covet them in your heart. If God has not provided you with the same possessions as your neighbor, you cannot desire them in your heart. When you do, you open up room for Satan to destroy you.
5. **Marriage:** A holy union honors God greatly. However, if your desire to marry causes you to have unholy affections for someone who is not returning your affections or toward the spouse of another, cut off the soul tie quickly before Satan has ground in your life.
6. **Television:** There is nothing sinful about watching TV or movies. However, "binge" watching is a form of dissipation. We are to make the best use of our time (Ephesians 5:15-16). Plus, many shows promote sin, aggrandize violence, and propagate unrighteous views of the world. Limit your TV time. Put no ungodly thing before your eyes (Psalm 101:3).

7. **Perversions:** A perversion is an unholy affection that rebels against the teachings of God and His righteous standards. Lusting after someone of the opposite sex is akin to adultery, but lusting after someone of the same sex is a perversion because it goes against the natural order. This includes cross-dressing, homosexuality, sodomy, lesbianism, gender confusion, bestiality, necrophilia, orgies, and other unclean practices. You must cut these unholy passions at the root. Soul ties with these kinds of demonic forces are difficult to break. But nothing is impossible with God.

8. **Pornography:** Viewing images of naked men or women is a doorway to great demonic influence. The lust opens doors to sins that can lead to every kind of perversion and sexual immortality. You must break all ties with pornographic images online, in magazines, and videos. Destroy and burn these destructive elements immediately. If you must, get rid of your computer. Jesus says, *"If your right eye causes you to sin, pluck it out and cast it from you; for it is more profitable for you that one of your members perish, than for your whole body to be cast into hell"* (Matthew 5:29).

9. **Relationships:** Any relationship (or lack of relationship) can open up an ungodly affection. All relationships must submit to the Law of God and the Lordship of Christ. Give all of your relationships to Christ so that no ungodly soul ties occur.

10. **Celebrities:** If you greatly esteem a celebrity, have their posters on your wall, and feel a special draw to them, you could be opening yourself up to demonic activity. These celebrities might even be "godly" men or women. However, trusting even a celebrity pastor or teacher above God can unleash satanic delusions that can keep you in bondage from trusting the pure Word of God. Don't have unholy affections for any celebrity, including TV stars, movie stars, musicians, artists, actors and actresses, civil leaders, sports players, church leaders, or any man or woman. If anyone has "celebrity status" in your heart, take note and break that soul tie.

Ungodly affections can open you up to a host of heartache and pain. Turn these passions off immediately. As soon as you notice some unholy desire rising in your heart, call out to Jesus for grace. James warns of the dangers of unholy affections: *"Adulterers and adulteresses! Do you not know that friendship with the world is enmity with God? Whoever therefore wants to be a friend of the world makes himself an enemy of God. Or do you think that the Scripture says in vain, 'The Spirit who dwells in us yearns jealously?'"* And then he provides the answer: *"But He gives more grace"* (James 4:4-6).

Call out to Jesus for grace to resist every unrighteous affection so that you never experience being "given up" to your vile passions.

HOMEWORK

Answer the following questions:

1. What does it mean for God to give someone up to their vile passions?

2. What is God's ultimate goal for giving a believer over to their sinful passions?

3. Explain how something "good" can be turned into an ungodly affection.

4. Which of the 10 affections listed above are never good?

5. Which affections in your life do you need to be careful about? Which do you need to sever immediately? Take whatever steps are necessary to break those ungodly affections.

6. Pray the prayers on the following page.

PRAYERS

1. Father, I do not want to be given over to vile passions.
2. Reveal any wicked affection in me, Lord, and remove it.
3. I ask that You apply the blood of Jesus Christ to all my areas of weakness, Lord. Heal me.
4. Take my legitimate affections, Lord, and help me not use them for an opportunity to sin against You.
5. Grant me the power to resist my sinful desires and the ploys of the devil who wants to keep me in bondage to sin.
6. Lord, I want to be Your friend. Help me to keep your commandments.
7. You are a jealous God. Keep all my affections godly, in Jesus' name.
8. I need Your grace to overcome my sin. Please, give me more grace.
9. Father, help me put no unclean thing before my eyes. Let me behold Your face alone.
10. Take away from me every vile passion, all ungodly affections, and each unholy desire so Satan cannot bring death and destruction into my life. Let me life honor You alone, in Jesus' name. Amen.

DAY TWENTY-THREE

SOUL TIES AND SIN

"Be angry, and do not sin": do not let the sun go down on your wrath, nor give place to the devil.
EPHESIANS 4:26-27

Have you noticed how society seems to have taken a nose-dive toward disease, sin, and corruption?

- Divorce rates are up
- Chronic illnesses are on the rise
- New diseases are crippling society
- People are growing cold toward weaker members of society
- Businesses are failing
- The economy is tanking

All these "symptoms" are listed in the Bible as "curses" toward men and societies that refuse to follow God's laws. Breaking the commandments of God (i.e., sinning) is the most common source of an ungodly soul tie. When we disobey God in any manner, we are opening ourselves up to Satanic soul ties through curses that God uses to discipline His children.

Sin and Cursing

Many people wrongly assume that God's commandments are burdensome, harsh, and take away all our fun. In reality, God's heart is just the opposite. He desires to give us an abundant life. Jesus said, *"I have come that they may have life, and that they may have it more abundantly."* In that same verse, Jesus reveals that it is the devil who wants to make life difficult for us: *"The thief does not come except to steal, and to kill, and to destroy"* (John 10:10).

God's laws are good. He has given them to us for our GOOD and our SURVIVAL: *"And the*

Lord commanded us to observe all these statutes, to fear the Lord our God, for our good always, that He might preserve us alive, as it is this day" (Deuteronomy 6:25).

Satan understands these principles full well. He knows that if he can "trick" someone into thinking sin is good and fun, then he can bring harm and death into their life instead. And the devil can do it with God's permission. Sin is basically giving Satan permission to bring destruction into our lives. Life and blessing come through obedience; and death and cursing come through sin. *"I call heaven and earth as witnesses today against you, that I have set before you life and death, blessing and cursing; therefore choose life, that both you and your descendants may live"* (Deuteronomy 30:19).

When we choose to sin, we open up spiritual portals that allow the demonic realm to bring about all the curses mentioned in Deuteronomy 28:15-68. *"But it shall come to pass, if you do not obey the voice of the Lord your God, to observe carefully all His commandments and His statutes which I command you today, that all these curses will come upon you and overtake you."* Below are a few of the curses you can open yourself up to if you are walking in rebellion to God's Law:

1. Curses in your town and city, food supply, offspring, wealth, and livelihood (16-18)
2. Difficulties and dangers when traveling (19)
3. Confusion, frustration of plans, and death (20)
4. Clinging plagues, consumption, illness, inflammation, mildew (21-22)
5. Bronze heaven, iron earth, and draught leading to death (23-24)
6. Your enemies will triumph over you (25)
7. Boils, tumors, cancer, skin conditions, itches that cannot be healed (27)
8. Madness, blindness, and confusion of heart (28)
9. Failure, oppression, and plundering (29)
10. Divorce, adultery, and unfruitful labors (30)
11. Children stolen from you while you watch on helpless (32)
12. Wicked leaders will rule over you (36)
13. People will deride you (37)
14. Pestilence on your crops (42)
15. Others will be exalted and you will be torn down (43)
16. You will be in debt and lose preeminence (44)
17. Destruction will overtake you (45)
18. You will serve your enemies (48)
19. Hunger, thirst, nakedness, great need, and a yoke of iron around your neck (48)
20. Rulers will not respect the elderly nor the young (50)

21. Destruction, cannibalism, loss of natural affections, (52-53)
22. Extraordinary plagues—great and prolonged plagues—and serious and prolonged sicknesses (59)
23. All the diseases of Egypt (60)
24. Every sickness and plague not mentioned in the Bible (61)
25. Decreasing influence (62)
26. Loss of home and property (63)
27. You will fall into idolatry and find no rest, (64-65)
28. Fear of death will consume you, trembling heart, failing eyes, and anguish of soul (65-66)
29. Your eyes will see atrocities you never dreamt of (67)
30. You will be sold into slavery, but no one will want to buy you (68)

"Moreover all these curses shall come upon you and pursue and overtake you, until you are destroyed, because you did not obey the voice of the Lord your God, to keep His commandments and His statutes which He commanded you. And they shall be upon you for a sign and a wonder, and on your descendants forever" (Deuteronomy 28:45-46).

Friends, anything on the above list is fair game to Satan if you do not obey the commandments of God. You should be trembling in your chair. Don't make the mistake of believing that these curses only applied to the Old Testament saints or the nation of Israel. Jesus says if we love Him, we will obey Him. *"For this is the love of God, that we keep His commandments. And His commandments are not burdensome* (1 John 5:3).

Obedience still brings blessings: *But without faith it is impossible to please Him, for he who comes to God must believe that He is, and that He is a rewarder of those who diligently seek Him* (Hebrews 11:6). And disobedience still brings cursing and opens doorways for Satan to establish a satanic soul tie in your life. The devil will take every opportunity. *"Be sober, be vigilant; because your adversary the devil walks about like a roaring lion, seeking whom he may devour"* (1 Peter 5:8).

All the curses listed above are bad news for believers who choose to walk in disobedience to the commands of God. However, God has made a way to break the power of these curses: and His name is Jesus Christ. Remember, Jesus broke the curse of the Law. Death has no power over you. But God will give Satan the right to torment you so that you will turn back to Him. *"Deliver such a one to Satan for the destruction of the flesh, that his spirit may be saved in the day of the Lord Jesus"* (1 Corinthians 5:5).

Tomorrow, and over the next couple of days, we are going to explore some difficult manifestations of ungodly soul ties. Today, consider that God has set before you blessings and curses, life and death. What will you choose?

HOMEWORK

Answer the following questions:

1. Why did God give us directions on how to live?

2. In what ways are you attracted to sin?

3. Can you see any potential outpouring of curses in your life? List them.

4. How can you break free from the curse of sin?

5. Explain the different motives behind God's desire for you to obey and Satan's desire for you to disobey.

6. Pray the prayers on the following page.

PRAYERS

1. Father, help me always remember that Satan is a liar.
2. Thank You for giving Your commandments for my good always and my survival.
3. I want the abundant life You have for me. Help me turn more and more from sin.
4. Lord, don't allow Satan to have ground in my life due to my sin. Cleanse me, Lord.
5. Father, give me such a love for Your Law that I'd seek to apply it everywhere.
6. You bring blessings for obedience, Lord. Help me access every blessing in Christ.
7. Reveal every wicked way in me. I confess I am a sinner, Lord. Forgive me of all my sins.
8. Father in heaven, hallowed be Your name. Your kingdom come. Your will be done on earth as it is in heaven.
9. Forgive me my sins as I forgive those who sin against me.
10. Lead me not into temptation but deliver me from the evil one. Yours is the kingdom, and the power, and the glory forever. Amen.

DAY TWENTY-FOUR

DEMONIC INTROJECTION

Do not be deceived: "Evil company corrupts good habits."
1 Corinthians 15:33

In days One through Twenty-Four, we defined and identified ungodly soul ties and provided the legal ground for you to have victory over all Satanic influences in your life. For the remainder of our 40-day journey, we will grapple with some manifestations of ungodly soul ties, the cords that bind them, and methods to break free from them forever so you can enjoy life the way God intended. Plus, we will look at how to form soul ties and relationships in your life that honor God and bring joy. Today, we are going to explore a manifestation of demonic soul ties called introjection.

What Is Introjection?

The word "introjection" is frequently used in the study of psychology and the mind. It means that a person unconsciously takes on characteristics, actions, or even thoughts from another person or entity. First, the person identifies a particular behavior, often without noticing, then incorporates it into their own repertoire of actions. A simple example is when you start to use the same words or gestures as your friends without recognizing why. It can come directly from another person, a group, or the general activities in the surrounding environment.

The psychological term "projection" is related to this process. Projection is when someone assigns thoughts or actions to someone else because they themselves have them. For example, you say someone is acting guilty because you feel guilty about something yourself. Introjection and projection happen commonly in daily life. However, something similar can manifest in the spiritual realm.

What Is Demonic Introjection?

A "demonic introjection" occurs when demonic forces infiltrate a person's soul, mind, or life so the person takes on characteristics of that demon. Perhaps you've noticed how people engaged in specific sins have similar personality characteristics. For example, a male homosexual might lisp, act effeminate, or use bodily gestures that identify their sexual orientation.

In this process, the demon takes on the role of an "introject" by intruding upon a person's soul, interjecting their personality characteristics onto the person. This process is a form of demonic possession that can occur when the subject does not live and act as God intends. The moment a person turns away from God's definition of right or wrong and chooses to behave contrary to God's revealed will, they invite demonic introjection.

Sin and Introjection

Any sin can open a pathway into your soul that allows introjects (demonic influences) into your mind and body. In the process, ungodly soul ties can be created or strengthened. Sinful unions, damaging or toxic relationships, and unequal yoking are invitations for this kind of demonic bondage. The Bible repeatedly warns, *"Do not be unequally yoked together with unbelievers. For what fellowship has righteousness with lawlessness? And what communion has light with darkness?"* (2 Corinthians 6:14).

If you have a great need for acceptance, camaraderie, kinship, or love — and are seeking it apart from Christ — you are at risk for demonic introjection. You will have to work extra hard to cut the cords and create new desires in your heart by renewing your mind. This is what we will be doing over the next several days. Now, let's look at some specific ways introjects can break into your life through sin.

Doorways to Introjection

Sin has many expressions. Introjection can come about from your own sins, the sins of others, or your own sinful responses to those who have harmed you. Below are some circumstances that can lead to demonic introjection in your life.

1. Soul Wounds
2. False Identity

3. Lying
4. Unforgivingness
5. Negative Emotions
6. Anger/Hatred
7. Fear
8. Depression
9. Pride
10. Grief
11. Sexual Sin
12. Ungodly Soul Ties
13. Being Unequally Yoked
14. Assault, Rape, and Molestation
15. Psychological Problems

As mentioned, not everything on the above list is due to your sin. Grief, for example, may not be the result of anyone's particular sin, but rather sin in general, since death entered the world through sin. Crimes against you, while not your fault, are the sin of another. And if you take on a victim mentality or refuse to forgive, then it leads to further sin. Psychological problems are very complex and may or may not include sin on your part. Yet, all these can be doorways to demonic introjection. And by God's grace, we can slam the door shut on them just as well.

The Harm of Introjection

We know that Satan has come only to kill, steal, and destroy. So what are the demonic plans against you through introjection? Let's explore a few ideas. Demonic introjection seeks to:

1. Keep you in bondage to your sin so you cannot enjoy godly relationships
2. Steal your identity by separating your soul into two or more conflicting parts
3. Create conflict in your life that leads to negative emotions and sinful actions
4. Lead you further down the path of destruction
5. Bind your hands from being fruitful in life and for Christ's Kingdom

Never, ever despair. God has provided everything you need to break free from the toxic chains of the devil. In previous chapters, we've mentioned many ways to break free from the bondage of sin and Satan. But, it is always good to repeat, remember, and refocus.

How to Break Free

Apply these seven steps to your life to break free from the demonic bonds of introjection.

1. Submit your life to the Lordship of Jesus Christ.
2. Repent and believe the gospel.
3. Renounce all sinful activities.
4. Engage in fasting, prayers, and other dedicated godly activities.
5. Accept Christ's provision and protection in faith.
6. Study and apply God's Word to all of life.
7. Put on the full armor of God.

Faith-Building Scripture

Before moving on to the homework, study the following Scriptures. These passages are hand chosen so you can grow in your faith.

- **Psalm 18:44-45:** *"As soon as they hear of me they obey me; the foreigners submit to me. The foreigners fade away and come frightened from their hideouts."*
- **Luke 10:19:** *"Behold, I give you the authority to trample on serpents and scorpions, and over all the power of the enemy, and nothing shall by any means hurt you."*
- **Deut. 7:15:** *"And the LORD will take away from you all sickness and will afflict you with none of the terrible diseases of Egypt which you have known, but will lay them on all those who hate you."*
- **Matthew 15:13:** *"But He answered and said, 'Every plant which My heavenly Father has not planted will be uprooted.'"*
- **James 4:7:** *"Therefore submit to God. Resist the devil and he will flee from you."*
- **Isaiah 54:17:** *"'No weapon formed against you shall prosper, And every tongue with rises against you in judgment You shall condemn. This is the heritage of the servants of the Lord, And their righteousness is from Me,' Says the Lord."*
- **2 Chronicles 20:6:** *"O Lord God of our fathers, are You not God in heaven, and do You not rule over all the kingdoms of the nations, and in Your hand is there not power and might, so that no one is able to withstand You?"*

HOMEWORK

Answer the following questions:

1. What is demonic introjection?

2. Can you identify any examples of introjection in your life or the life of others? Please describe.

3. What is the harm of introjection?

4. What doorways in your life may allow demonic introjection in your life?

5. What steps do you need to take immediately to close doorways to introjection?

6. Pray the prayers on the following page.

PRAYERS

1. In the name of Jesus, I close all doorways to demonic introjection in my life.
2. I renounce all sinful relationships and agree to break them off immediately.
3. Father, remove all Satanic forces trying to introject themselves into my life.
4. I refuse to be a victim and will hold no grudges against those who have harmed me.
5. I confess my sins of pride, unforgivingness, and anger, in Jesus' name.
6. God in heaven, I submit my life to the Lordship of Jesus Christ.
7. I believe the good news that Jesus paid for my sins, and I renounce all sin in my life.
8. Clothe me in the full armor of God so that I can stand against the schemes of the devil.
9. In Your holy name, I accept Christ's provision and protection from all demonic activity.
10. I am fully accepted by Jesus and will live my life for Him alone.

DAY TWENTY-FIVE

SOUL FRAGMENTATION

*He restores my soul; He leads me in the paths of
righteousness For His name's sake.*
PSALM 23:3

Have you ever helped a friend through a grieving process when their parent or spouse passes away? You may have noticed the one grieving appears lifeless and "dead" themselves for a while as they struggle to pull their life back together. You may have even experienced this type of loss yourself and understand exactly how your everyday activities end up feeling mechanical. You go through the motions, but have no cognitive control over them. You feel numb to the world.

Our bodies have many techniques to help us overcome difficult times. Sometimes, our coping mechanisms can be extremely harmful to the soul, even causing fragmentation. Let's take a look at one of these coping tools.

Suppressing Harmful Memories

People who experience extreme stress, traumatic events, or particularly challenging times often cope by suppressing the harmful memories. This suppression of real-life events can cause a soul fragmentation where the inner self separates into one or more parts so they can function in day-to-day life. However, the broken pieces in the soul need expression and will come to the surface in tangible ways. When this happens, someone may unexpectedly find themselves unhappy, overwrought, empty, or in anguish and not even know why. Soul fragmentation makes it impossible to continue a healthy and joy-filled existence.

When this type of fragmenting occurs, you can experience a wide variety of negative issues and emotions that affect you spiritually, physically, emotionally, financially, and relationally. Many people with soul fragmentation state that they feel empty inside or like something has been lost from their life.

Mind, Will, and Emotions

Your soul (or person) consists of three basic components: the mind, will, and emotions. This can be seen by looking at how the Bible speaks of the soul.

1. **The Soul Is the Mind:** Knowledge and understanding begin in the mind. This knowledge resides in the soul. Therefore, the mind is part of the soul. Psalms 139:14: *"I will praise You, for I am fearfully and wonderfully made; Marvelous are Your works, And that my **soul knows** very well."*
2. **The Soul Is the Emotions:** The Bible also demonstrates that our feelings and emotions also reside in the soul. Psalms 35:9: *"And my **soul** shall be **joyful** in the LORD: it shall **rejoice** in His salvation."*
3. **The Soul Is the Will:** Our decisions are made in our soul as well. Job 7:14-15: *"Then You scare me with dreams And terrify me with visions, So that my **soul chooses** strangling And death rather than my body."*

Since the soul consists of mind, will, and emotions, soul fragmentation can occur in any or every part of your being, affecting how you think, feel, and act. Let's look at some symptoms.

Symptoms of Soul Fragmentation

Below are some potential manifestations of soul fragmentation in your life:

- Sorrow, depression, foreboding, or a sense of loss
- Difficulty making decisions, confusion, or lack of clarity
- Loss of purpose or focus, difficulty sleeping, fatigue, or malaise
- Withdrawal from the world and godly relationships
- Unfounded fears and anxiety
- Feeling numb or without the energy to do anything
- Making decisions that hurt you physically, emotionally, spiritually, or financially

These symptoms may come and go, last a short time, or continues for years if the soul is not healed by God's grace. The longer you wait to heal your fragmented soul, the more your behaviors, thoughts, and words, will become increasingly distorted and difficult to bear. You must take action to put your fragmented soul back together again.

Since many difficulties in the mind, will, and emotions result from a fragmented soul, restoration can resolve many life struggles. Soul fragment recovery involves binding your soul back together with God's love and power. Thus, it recreates you as a whole godly being with an intact soul. "*Therefore, if anyone is in Christ, he is a new creation; old things have passed away; behold, all things have become new*" (2 Corinthians 5:17).

Trauma and Abuse

People who undergo considerable trauma such as a violent attack or accident may lose their sense of self and retreat into a type of mindless forward motion. Abuse victims often dissociate from the horrific things they experience and cannot find the power to escape. Even if they do, they may feel as if they were torn apart by the process.

Below are some deeper and more specific expressions of soul fragmentation from abuse or trauma.

- The feeling that you are missing some important part of yourself
- Breaks in memory, especially of childhood or another traumatic time
- Depression that lasts a long time after the triggering circumstance is over
- Missing a part of yourself that can help bring you joy
- Seeking out extreme situations and experiences in an attempt to regain the feeling of control or invigoration lost with the soul piece
- Ongoing physical maladies, lack of energy, illness, and disorder not caused by normal medical issues
- An overall feeling of lack of fulfillment and joy in your life
- Emotional numbness or inability to feel normal emotions like happiness or love
- Difficulty sleeping for extended periods or the desire to do nothing but sleep
- The impression that you have changed or become intrinsically different after undergoing a particularly difficult experience
- Inability to move forward with your life or take steps to improve your situation
- The belief that you are not worthy of love, true friendship, or good things
- A sense of plodding through life's daily activities without real purpose
- Protecting yourself from future harm by not allowing others into your life or heart
- A general view that you lack control over your own life and actions
- Escapism through entertainment, excess work, addiction, or meaningless relationships and sex

- Fatigue, mental exhaustion, and lethargy not caused by illness
- A hunger for acceptance, a striving for purpose, or a desire to live an authentic life

If you recognize any of the above symptoms, your fragmented soul needs healing.

More Causes of Fragmentation

Below are some additional reasons why people suffer from soul fragmentation.

- Children are abandoned by parents or mistreated by their caregivers
- Constant arguments or conflict in the home
- Extreme injuries or emotional distress due to a house fire, vehicle crash, or another traumatic event
- Comas, chronic illness, or life-threatening conditions or diseases
- Divorce, death, or other life-changing events
- Sexual abuse, rape, or participation in satanic rituals

The grief and struggle to regain normalcy after these and other events often come with soul fragmentation. Many people who experience mild types of fragmentations can recover on their own. However, those who have gone through more extreme trauma have no power to escape these issues. All people ultimately desire to have whole souls and the ensuing energy and vitality that brings a strong purpose in life leading to joy and fulfillment. Those with fragmented souls must call upon the Lord to heal and restore them. This is the only way.

A Prayer for Healing

Father, I ask You in the Name of Jesus Christ to send out angels to gather up the fragments of my soul and restore them to their rightful place in my life by Your mighty power (Psalm 7:2, 23:3).

With the full power and authority of the Lord Jesus, I ask that you send every help I need to heal my broken heart, bind my wounds, give me a sound mind, restore proper emotions, and teach me to do Your will on earth as it is in heaven.

Restore all the pieces of my fragmented mind, will, emotions, appetite, intellect, heart, finances, flesh, and personality. Bring them all into proper balance and to the original position where they belong in Christ Jesus.

Lord Jesus Christ, please command Satan and all of his demons to release my mind completely. I ask You, Father, to send Your angels to break, cut, and sever all fetters, bands, chains, ties, and bonds of whatever sort the enemy has managed to place on my mind by word or deed. Bestow unto me and my family every spiritual blessing in Christ: Wisdom, Counsel, Might, Knowledge, Fear of the Lord, Power, Love, Sound Mind, Grace, Peace, and the Fruit of the Spirit. Thank You for answering, in Jesus' name, Amen.

HOMEWORK

Answer the following questions:

1. What is soul fragmentation?

2. Are you experiencing any of the symptoms of soul fragmentation? List them.

3. Which events in your life might cause fragmentation of your soul?

4. How can you be healed of soul fragmentation (draw from any previous chapters if needed)?

5. Memorize 2 Timothy 1:7: *"For God has not given us a spirit of fear, but of power and of love and of a sound mind."* Ask God to give you a sound mind.

6. Pray the prayers on the following page.

PRAYERS

1. In the name of Jesus, I acknowledge that God has given me a sound mind.
2. Restore my soul and lead me in the paths of righteousness for Your name's sake.
3. I accept the healing promised by the power of God to restore my soul.
4. Father, take my mind, will, and emotions and bind them together in You.
5. Restore every missing or hiding piece of my soul with Your presence, Lord.
6. Help me find wholeness in my soul through Your mighty power.
7. Heal me, Lord, and I will be healed. Restore me, and I will be restored.
8. Search my heart, Lord, for any hidden hurt, trauma, abuse, abandonment, or any other source of soul fragmentation in my life.
9. Help me face the source of fragmentation head-on and without fear so You can heal me, Lord.
10. I accept full healing in my soul, Lord. Thank You for desiring the best for me. I trust You, in Jesus' name.

DAY TWENTY-SIX

SOUL WOUNDS

*I said, "Lord, be merciful to me; Heal my soul,
for I have sinned against You."*
PSALM 41:4

Yesterday, we discussed how our soul is made up of mind, will, and emotions. The soul is also closely related to our hearts and includes our conscience. In the Bible, the word "heart" is sometimes used as a synonym for the soul. The words can be used interchangeably. Just as the physical heart pumps blood around your body with four chambers, when we add the conscience into the mix, we see that our soul also has four chambers: mind, will, emotions, and conscience.

The four chambers of the heart must work in perfect harmony to have a healthy soul. When one part is wounded, all parts of the body malfunction. Today, we are going to look at a very significant soul wound: the wounded conscience.

The God Conscience

Every person is born with a conscious awareness of the existence of God. The Bible declares that *"what may be known of God is manifest in them, for God has shown it to them. For since the creation of the world His invisible attributes are clearly seen, being understood by the things that are made, even His eternal power and Godhead, so that they are without excuse* (Romans 1:19-20). No one can say they didn't know that God exists. The knowledge of God is written on their hearts.

Plus, even though men know God exists, they willingly choose to live contrary to His ways. *"Although they knew God, they did not glorify Him as God, nor were thankful, but became futile in their thoughts, and their foolish hearts were darkened"* (Romans 1:32). The result of rejecting God is a soul wound so severe that it leads to eternal damnation. This kind of sin is against their own souls (Number 16:38), and it leads to death (Romans 6:23) and eternal damnation (Revelation 20:15). This is the state of all men who reject Christ as Lord.

Soul Cleansing

To escape the natural consequences of this most devastating soul wound, the conscience must be purified. *"Let us draw near with a true heart in full assurance of faith, having our hearts sprinkled from an evil conscience and our bodies washed with pure water"* (Hebrews 10:22).

Before we can be delivered from the outside forces of evil, we must first cleanse that which resides inside our hearts. We must be born again. Once you undergo the true process of being born again, you have power over all the demonic forces that prey on your spirit. The Holy Spirit can and will heal all ungodly wounds and demonic influences. But first, the heart must be renewed. All soul wounds originate from turning away from God or rejecting His teachings. Soul wounds may also happen if you believe God has forsaken you.

Forsaking and Feeling Forsaken

Some people seem to pray fervently for salvation and God's grace, yet do not receive it. In these cases, it is often because they have rejected God in some way. It may be that they feel they have been rejected by God. Yet, God promises that He will not reject anyone who draws near to Him in faith (James 4:8). Unfortunately, people who feel forsaken actually lack faith and reject the truth of God's Word. When Satan or other ungodly forces infiltrate your life, you can wrongly believe that God has turned away from you, even if it is not true.

If you feel abandoned by God, ask forgiveness, repent, and believe. Pray with your whole heart, asking for more grace to believe. If you lack faith, ask God to grant it to you just as the disciples did: *"And the apostles said to the Lord, "Increase our faith"* (Luke 17:5). Also, acknowledge your unbelief, confessing it as sin. Some people find it quite challenging to humble themselves in this way and ask for repentance when they feel abandoned or wronged.

Guilty Conscience

Unconfessed sin leads to another great soul wound: the guilty conscience. In our souls, we all know that sin is wrong and deserves to be punished. When sin remains unconfessed it leads to a guilty conscience. While we may try to suppress the guilt, it will manifest in various ways, including further sin, avoidance of people, physical ailments, lack of devotion to God, depression, and other ways.

Consider the words of David when he had a guilty conscience: *"When I kept silent, my bones grew old through my groaning all the day long. For day and night Your hand was heavy upon me; My vitality was turned into the drought of summer"* (Psalm 32:3-4). Don't allow a guilty conscience to would your soul. *"I said, 'I will confess my transgressions to the Lord,' And You forgave the iniquity of my sin"* (Psalm 32:5). If you continually attempt to suppress your guilt, it will lead to a seared conscience. Confess your sin, and God will forgive you.

Seared Conscience

Sadly, when sin is left unconfessed, it leads to a seared conscience, which is a strong indication a person is not born again. When a person refuses to listen to the Holy Spirit's warnings about sin, God will give them over to their sin so they no longer feel guilty. *"Now the Spirit expressly says that in latter times some will depart from the faith, giving heed to deceiving spirits and doctrines of demons, speaking lies in hypocrisy, having their own conscience seared with a hot iron"* (1 Timothy 4:1-2).

If the Bible calls something sin (like sexual immorality), yet a person willingly continues in it without guilt, that person is in danger of hellfire. If that describes you, it is very possible God has given you over to your sin and your conscience is seared. Repent immediately while there is still time. *"Beware, brethren, lest there be in any of you an evil heart of unbelief in departing from the living God; but exhort one another daily, while it is called 'Today,' lest any of you be hardened through the deceitfulness of sin"* (Hebrews 3:12-13).

False Healing

Soul wounds can also be caused by someone sinning against you. For example, if you take guilt upon yourself when someone else has sinned against you, it can lead to the same negative effects mentioned above, including a guilty or seared conscience. Confess any involvement on your part, even if it is just feeling guilty for something you did not do (a form of lying). Ask God to heal you.

In extreme cases of trauma, wounded souls can seek to heal themselves falsely by fragmenting. This can lead to what is known as multiple personality disorder, bipolar disorder, and schizophrenia. These "psychotic breaks" due to extreme trauma can shatter your self into multiple pieces. The Bible warns: *"a double-minded man [is] unstable in all his ways"* (James 1:8). If you have built a wall of faux defense, give it over to Jesus. These methods will not heal your soul; only Christ can do that.

True Healing

True healing only comes through Jesus Christ. Apply these principles to your life to heal your soul wounds.

1. **Seek God:** Ask the Holy Spirit to help you get to the root of your soul wounds so you can begin the healing process.
2. **Study Scripture:** Dig deep into God's Word to learn how to recover from fear, pain, rejections, and trauma.
3. **Search Your Heart:** Look inward to honestly evaluate unconfessed sins you need to repent of. *"Search me, O God, and know my heart; Try me, and know my anxieties"* (Psalm 139:23).
4. **Sever Ungodly Soul Ties**: Apply the resources in this book to remove and destroy all ungodly soul ties in your life, especially those that involved sinful or traumatic events.
5. **Seal Your Fragmented Soul:** Take all the necessary steps to restore your fragmented soul and recover the sound mind that God has designed for you.
6. **Shatter Satan's Power:** Make use of the full power of God to kick Satan and his demons out of your life.
7. **Speak Victory:** Believe God and declare that He can, has, and will deliver you completely from all soul wounds in Jesus' name.

Bible Verses to Heal the Soul

To get you started on step two above, we've included some verses to meditate upon and memorize. Some are preventive medicine, others promises of healing, and still others are healing salve for damaged souls. No matter, they will bring health to your bones and healing to your soul.

- **Psalm 41:4:** *"I said, 'Lord, be merciful to me; Heal my soul, for I have sinned against You.'"*
- **Psalm 23:3:** *"He restores my soul; He leads me in the paths of righteousness for His name's sake."*
- **Proverbs 6:32:** *"Whoever commits adultery with a woman lacks understanding; He who does so destroys his own soul."*
- **Proverbs 17:22:** *"A merry heart does good, like medicine, But a broken spirit dries the bones."*
- **Proverbs 15:13:** *"A merry heart makes a cheerful countenance, but by sorrow of the heart the spirit is broken."*

- **Psalm 147:3:** "*He heals the brokenhearted and binds up their wounds.*"
- **Proverbs 16:24:** "*Pleasant words are like a honeycomb, Sweetness to the soul and health to the bones.*"
- **3 John 1:2:** "*Beloved, I pray that you may prosper in all things and be in health, just as your soul prospers.*"
- **Exodus 15:26:** "*If you diligently heed the voice of the Lord your God and do what is right in His sight, give ear to His commandments and keep all His statutes, I will put none of the diseases on you which I have brought on the Egyptians. For I am the Lord who heals you.*"

HOMEWORK

Answer the following questions:

1. Why are soul wounds so dangerous?

2. List three kinds of soul wounds that involve the conscience.

3. What is the cure for a guilty conscience?

4. List any sins in your life that put you in danger of a seared conscience. Confess them and forsake them immediately.

5. What are the seven steps to heal soul wounds?

6. Pray the prayers on the following page.

PRAYERS

1. Father, I don't want to reject or refuse You in any way; increase my faith.
2. Make Your ways known to me, Lord.
3. Please reveal to me any hidden sins so I can confess and forsake them.
4. Please do not give me over to a seared conscience.
5. Shatter Satan's power in my life, and restore my soul.
6. Please do not let me seek false methods of healing.
7. I look to You alone for healing, Lord, for You are my healer. I know you will heal me.
8. Lord, if there is any hidden way in me, lack of faith, or another soul wound in my life, reveal it and heal it, in Jesus' name.
9. Be merciful to me Lord. Forgive my sins, and heal my wounds.
10. Father, cause my soul to prosper in all ways, in Jesus' name. Amen.

DAY TWENTY-SEVEN

SEVER UNGODLY SOUL TIES

*For this reason, a man will leave his mother and be united
to his wife, and they will become one flesh.*
GENESIS 2:24

It is time to sever the ungodly soul ties. God, our Creator and Designer, knows how we function best. If we want to know how to have a productive, fulfilled life, we should go to Him for instructions. We can trust Him. And from the beginning, God created humans as "male" and "female," and said, *"For this reason a man shall leave his father and mother and be joined to his wife, and the two shall become one flesh. So then, they are no longer two but one flesh"* (Matthew 19:5-6).

When the Bible records marriages that go against His perfect design, it also reveals the ensuing turmoil: Leah felt unloved; Rachel was jealous; Hannah grieved because her rival had children and she did not; Solomon's heart turned to idolatry. God's way is always best: one man for one woman for life.

The Breakdown

In modern society, even among professing believers, sexual immorality is rampant. As a result, prior to marriage, a man or woman may have engaged in sexual relations with multiple partners.

Besides breaking the commandments of God, having multiple sexual encounters causes another problem: each relationship creates a soul bond. The bond that was meant to be exclusively between husband and wife is now shared with others. *"Or do you not know that he who is joined to a harlot is one body with her? For 'the two,' He says, 'shall become one flesh'"* (1 Corinthians 6:16). Having multiple sexual partners causes a fragmentation of the soul that makes it difficult to join with one person exclusively in a loving bond.

If you have been joined to multiple partners, do not despair. You have the opportunity to break free from these destructive relationships and enjoy a new and more wonderful life by living according to the plans of your Creator. When you offer sincere repentance and ask God for forgiveness, He will forgive you and restore your soul. When He grants restoration, you can once more live with hope, love, and freedom. *"Create in me a clean heart, O God, and renew a right spirit within me"* (Psalms 51:10).

4 Steps to Break the Bonds

It is not hard to break the bonds of ungodly soul ties when you do it God's way. Below are four simple steps to begin breaking the ungodly soul ties in your life.

1. **Recognize and acknowledge the soul ties that exist in your life:** Admitting you have a problem is the most important step to solving it. Any turmoil within your heart and soul suggests there is an ungodly tie. Ask God to reveal the source of the soul tie.

2. **Confess your misdeeds and repent truly with your whole heart.** Next, honestly confess the sins of your past and genuinely turn from them. You may want to seek the help of a pastor, church elder, godly family member, or trustworthy Christian friend.

3. **Forgive those who have wronged you.** Forgiveness is more than a commandment; it is a healing tonic for your soul. Accept that God has the power to bestow it upon you.

    First, follow God's lead by forgiving yourself for your sins. The Apostle Paul was a great sinner, yet he wrote, *"Brethren, I do not count myself to have apprehended; but one thing I do, forgetting those things which are behind and reaching forward to those things which are ahead* (Philippians 3:13).

    Next, forgive [do not be bitter against] the people who were involved with the ungodly soul ties even if they were abusive or controlling. Consider these sobering words from St. Augustine: "Resentment is like drinking poison and waiting for the other person to die."

4. **Break away from the bonds, and destroy the ungodly soul ties.** Fourth, pray aloud to the Lord Jesus Christ, asking Him to destroy the ungodly soul ties. Implore Him with your voice to help you. There is power in the spoken word. *"Death and life are in the power of the tongue"* (Proverbs 18:21).

    It is also vital during this breaking away process, to throw away or destroy anything that reminds you of the person or ties you to them. This can include, cards, letters, gifts, clothing, jewelry, mementos, photographs, or any other thing that belongs to them or that they gave you.

Additional Tips to Destroy Ungodly Soul Ties

Below are five additional tips that work together with the steps above to help you break away from ungodly soul ties.

1. **Repent:** Confess and turn from any sins you committed while in the clutches of the ungodly soul tie. These may include fornication, telling lies, or anything else in violation of God's Law.

2. **Remove:** Get rid of all physical reminders of the past relationship. Burn letters, flowers, gifts, and more. If you cannot burn the objects, find another way to dispose of them completely.

3. **Renounce:** Disclaim all promises, vows, and contracts made while under the influence of the ungodly soul tie. This can include statements such as "We will be together forever" or "I give you my heart" or any other promise made during the good times in the relationship. *"Whoever guards his mouth and tongue keeps his soul from troubles"* (Proverbs 21:23). Also, repent of your role in forming the soul tie in Jesus' name.

4. **Resolve:** Commit to forgiving the person's transgressions against you and letting go of all hatred, resentment, pain, or bitterness in your heart toward the person. If you do not, it will poison your soul.

5. **Revoke:** In Jesus' name, fully renounce and revoke the ungodly soul tie and its hold on you and your life. Below are some sample prayers of revocation.

    Example #1: In Jesus' name I now renounce any and all ungodly soul ties created between myself and _____ as a result of _____ in Jesus' name.

    Example #2: In the name of the Lord Jesus Christ, I cancel, break, and renounce all relationships influenced by Satan and any wicked spirits between _____ and me.

Example #3: I renounce in Jesus' name any soul tie empowered by Satan, and I reject all efforts that the enemy has used to form and continue these relationships.

Example #4: I revoke all ungodly, destructive, and harmful effects this soul tie has caused for me (my marriage, my family, and my ministry), and I forbid any further intrusion or ongoing use of this relationship by the enemy against me and those I hold godly soul ties with. I petition the blessings and freedoms of my Lord Jesus. I proclaim this in the name and power of Lord Jesus Christ. Amen!

HOMEWORK

Answer the following questions:

1. Why can you trust God?

2. What are some consequences of ungodly soul ties?

3. List the four steps to break away from ungodly soul ties?

4. What are the five additional tips to break away?

5. Which of the four steps or five tips is most difficult for you and why?

6. Pray the prayers on the following page.

PRAYERS

1. Lord, I acknowledge the following sinful relationships in my life (name them).
2. Father, I repent of the sins I committed in my past relationships (name them).
3. Lord, I forgive _____ for hurting me in a past relationship.
4. Help me forgive _____ from my heart and refuse to hold bitterness or resentment toward them.
5. Help me see my sins in this relationship as behind me and look forward to the upward call in Christ.
6. Remind me of any tangible items I am holding on to from past relationships so I can immediately destroy them.
7. I renounce all promises and careless words tying me to any ungodly person in my life.
8. Deliver me, Lord, from all ungodly soul ties.
9. I cry to You, Lord, break me free from all of Satan's schemes to hold me in bondage, in Jesus' name.
10. I renounce any soul tie empowered by Satan, and I reject all efforts of the enemy to keep me tied to ungodly relationships, in Jesus' name. Amen!

DAY TWENTY-EIGHT

THE ACT OF FORGIVENESS

But if you do not forgive men their trespasses, neither will your Father forgive your trespasses.
MATTHEW 6:15

Unforgivingness is one sin that can destroy your relationships and keep you out of the Kingdom of heaven. Since forgiving others can be a great stumbling block for many people, we are going to spend the next two days looking at the two sides of forgiveness: receiving and giving. Both are required to enter the kingdom of heaven. For if you refuse to forgive those who trespass against you, neither will your Father forgive your trespasses (a requirement for eternal life). Today we will start with the hard side: forgiving others.

As We Forgive Our Debtors

Jesus tells a parable in Matthew 18:21-35 that perfectly illustrates the principle of forgiving others as God has forgiven us.

> Then Peter came to Him and said, "Lord, how often shall my brother sin against me, and I forgive him? Up to seven times?"
>
> Jesus said to him, "I do not say to you, up to seven times, but up to seventy times seven. Therefore the kingdom of heaven is like a certain king who wanted to settle accounts with his servants. And when he had begun to settle accounts, one was brought to him who owed him ten thousand talents. But as he was not able to pay, his master commanded that he be sold, with his wife and children and all that he had, and that payment be made. The servant therefore fell down before him, saying, 'Master, have

patience with me, and I will pay you all.' Then the master of that servant was moved with compassion, released him, and forgave him the debt.

"But that servant went out and found one of his fellow servants who owed him a hundred denarii; and he laid hands on him and took *him* by the throat, saying, 'Pay me what you owe!' So his fellow servant fell down at his feet and begged him, saying, 'Have patience with me, and I will pay you all.' And he would not, but went and threw him into prison till he should pay the debt. So when his fellow servants saw what had been done, they were very grieved, and came and told their master all that had been done. Then his master, after he had called him, said to him, 'You wicked servant! I forgave you all that debt because you begged me. Should you not also have had compassion on your fellow servant, just as I had pity on you?' And his master was angry, and delivered him to the torturers until he should pay all that was due to him.

"So My heavenly Father also will do to you if each of you, from his heart, does not forgive his brother his trespasses."

Our sin against a holy God is great in comparison with the sins that others commit against us. If we don't forgive others, Christ will not forgive us.

Jesus taught us to pray: Forgive us our debts (trespasses, sins) as we forgive our debtors (those who trespass or sin against us). If Christ has forgiven you for your many sins, you too ought to forgive others. *"But if you do not forgive men their trespasses, neither will your Father forgive your trespasses"* (Matthew 6:15). Are you struggling to forgive others? Consider the cost: your very soul.

Forgiving Others

It can be extremely difficult to forgive those who have trespassed against you, especially in destructive relationships. Below are some sins that are extremely hard to forgive because they cut so deep into your soul.

- **Slander:** When someone you care about spreads false information about you, it can be devastating. You may "feel" that you will never be able to face your friends, family, or co-workers again. However, what really matters is what God thinks of you. He knows the truth. Trust Him, and do not hold bitterness against the one who has harmed your reputation falsely.

- **Verbal Abuse:** The old saying, "Sticks and stones may break your bones, but words can never hurt you" is completely false. Words cut like knives and can do permanent damage to your soul, unless Christ heals you. Worse damage will be caused by holding resentment in your heart. To begin your healing, pray for those who have abused you with their tongue.
- **Physical Abuse:** Verbal abuse leaves scars in your heart, but physical abuse leaves scars in the heart and body. Don't let these reminders cause you to hold bitterness toward your abuser. Rather, release it to the Lord. Leave the vengeance up to Him.
- **Sexual Abuse:** Nothing could be worse than having intimacy taken by force. These wounds can easily prevent you from having a satisfying relationship with your spouse. Christ can heal you. Start by letting go of anger, bitterness, and thoughts of revenge toward your attacker. When forgiveness is complete, it will be a healing balm to your soul.
- **Lying:** When someone you care about lies to you, it can make you start distrusting all your relationships. Don't carry the grudge into your future. Let it go. Give each person their own chance to prove their loyalty. *"To the pure all things are pure, but to those who are defiled and unbelieving nothing is pure; but even their mind and conscience are defiled"* (Titus 1:15). Don't let someone else's sin defile you. Release it to the Lord.
- **Betrayal:** When a spouse or close friend cheats on you, speaks against your back, or seeks to destroy you, it can literally feel like you have been stabbed in the back. King Saul betrayed David, Judas betrayed Jesus, and Delilah betrayed Samsun. Each recovered from the betrayal in the power of the Spirit. Do not hold bitterness in your heart, but leave room for God to take revenge.
- **Stealing:** When someone you trust takes something that belongs to you, it can make you feel vulnerable and helpless. You may be angry and want to pay them back. Yet, the Bible says do not return *"evil for evil or reviling for reviling, but on the contrary blessing, knowing that you were called to this, that you may inherit a blessing"* (1 Peter 3:9). The blessing comes from letting go of all anger, bitterness, and wrath.

Forgiveness is not easy. If you are experiencing these behaviors in a current relationship, protect yourself by cutting the ties immediately. With past relationships, focus on letting go of your perceived right to bitterness. Yes, these things are wrong. You can even ask God to repay these people back according to His perfect righteousness. But you must let go of all bitterness towards those who have hurt you. Remember the words of St. Augustine: "Resentment is like drinking poison and waiting for the other person to die." You are the one who will suffer, not them.

True Forgiveness

There is a sense that you cannot fully forgive a person unless they confess their sins and ask you to forgive them. Yet, you can be perfectly healed in the relationship even if that never happens.

If the offense against you is not severe, you ought to go to the person and let them know they have offended you. Matthew 18:15-17 provides further instruction on this process. In cases of abuse, you may need to report the person to the proper civil authority. Seek counsel from a leader in your church who is trustworthy and full of wisdom.

When confession of sin is never made, you can still live in perfect peace. Follow these directions from the Apostle Paul: *"Let all bitterness, wrath, anger, clamor, and evil speaking be put away from you, with all malice. And be kind to one another, tenderhearted, forgiving one another, even as God in Christ forgave you"* (Ephesians 4:31-32). This is a work of the Spirit that may take time and prayer. Make it your goal.

Forgive Yourself

In all your forgiving of others, make sure you do not condemn yourself for the part you played in the sin of your past relationships. If you have sinned, confess it to the Lord. But do not let guilt and shame steal your joy. Once you have confessed your sins, God forgives you. Are you in a position to hold yourself to a higher standard than God? *"If we confess our sins, He is faithful and just to forgive us our sins and to cleanse us from all unrighteousness"* (1 John 1:9).

If you can forgive others, you can also forgive yourself. God does. Trust Him today and let go of your shame and guilt for your past mistakes.

HOMEWORK

Answer the following questions:

1. Are you struggling to forgive others?

2. List the specific sins and people you are struggling to forgive.

3. Why must you forgive those who sin against you?

4. What can happen to you if you do not forgive others?

5. Write down and meditate upon St. Augustine's quote about resentment.

6. Pray the prayers on the following page.

PRAYERS

1. Lord, help me forgive those who have trespassed against me.
2. Help me not return evil for evil or reviling for reviling, but instead a blessing, knowing that I was called to this, that I may inherit a blessing.
3. Father, I forgive_____ for _____. I let go of all bitterness toward them.
4. Lord, I entrust those who have hurt me into Your hands. Do with them as You choose.
5. I forgive all those who have used critical words against me or sinned against me in any way.
6. Please, Lord, forgive me for the resentment I have toward those who have hurt me.
7. Remove all bitterness, clamor, and slander far from me, Lord.
8. Father, heal all my wounds.
9. Help me live my life to its fullest by Your design.
10. Thank You for forgiving me of my many sins. Forgive my debts as I forgive my debtors.

DAY TWENTY-NINE

RECEIVING FORGIVENESS

*If we confess our sins, He is faithful and just to forgive us
our sins and to cleanse us from all unrighteousness.*
1 John 1:9

Today, we are going to look at the easier side of forgiveness: receiving it. Yet, this forgiveness did not come easy at all. Our sins can only be forgiven because of the cruel death of our Savior Jesus Christ. *"Yet it pleased the Lord to bruise Him"* (Isaiah 53:10). And Jesus, *"for the joy that was set before Him endured the cross, despising the shame, and has sat down at the right hand of the throne of God"* (Hebrews 12:2).

What was the joy set before Christ? His exaltation to the right hand of God to intercede on our behalf forever. *"Therefore He is also able to save to the uttermost those who come to God through Him, since He always lives to make intercession for them"* (Hebrews 7:25). Because of His death, resurrection, and exaltation, He saves sinners by interceding on their behalf to God.

Forgive Us Our Debts

God's ability to forgive us does not happen in a vacuum. It is impossible for God to "wink" at sin or excuse our wrong behavior. God is righteous and just, and will not leave the guilty unpunished (Exodus 34:7). This means that all sin must be punished. As we saw previously: *"the wages of sin is death"* (Romans 6:23). And God cannot lie. The only way for God to save sinners and reconcile them to Himself is through:

1. **Propitiation:** the act of fulfilling God's wrath, i.e., the guilty party paying the required penalty of death; and
2. **Substitutionary Atonement:** Jesus taking the penalty upon Himself by suffering death in our place and applying it to our account.

To simplify: Christ died in our place and took the punishment we deserved for our generational sin and our individual sins. When we trust that transaction in faith, God looks at us as if we have never sinned. Plus, He sees Christ's perfect righteousness instead of our filthy rags. That's how we are forgiven, but we must do our part. *"If we confess our sins, He is faithful and just to forgive us our sins and to cleanse us from all unrighteousness"* (1 John 1:9).

Prayers for Forgiveness in the Bible

Ultimately, all sin is against God and God alone. In a model prayer, David asks for forgiveness after engaging in sexual sin and murder. David prays:

> "Have mercy upon me, O God, According to Your lovingkindness; According to the multitude of Your tender mercies, Blot out my transgressions. Wash me thoroughly from my iniquity, And cleanse me from my sin. For I acknowledge my transgressions, And my sin is always before me. Against You, You only, have I sinned, And done this evil in Your sight—That You may be found just when You speak, And blameless when You judge" (Psalm 51:1-4).

In another prayer for forgiveness, Nehemiah acknowledges his guilt through covenantal sin and personal sin. Nehemiah's prayer:

> "I pray, Lord God of heaven, O great and awesome God, You who keep Your covenant and mercy with those who love You and observe Your commandments, please let Your ear be attentive and Your eyes open, that You may hear the prayer of Your servant which I pray before You now, day and night, for the children of Israel Your servants, and confess the sins of the children of Israel which we have sinned against You. Both my father's house and I have sinned. We have acted very corruptly against You, and have not kept the commandments, the statutes, nor the ordinances which You commanded Your servant Moses. Remember, I pray, the word that You commanded Your servant Moses, saying, 'If you are unfaithful, I will scatter you among the nations'" (Nehemiah 1:5-8).

Just like David and Nehemiah, we all stand guilty before God. We must go to Him for the only remedy for our sins.

ASKING FOR FORGIVENESS

To receive forgiveness, we must confess our sins before God and ask Him with a sincere heart to forgive us. First, we must confess in general that we are sinners. This acknowledgment is called *"repentance to life"* and accompanies genuine salvation (Acts 11:18). After that, we must continually ask God to forgive us for the sins we commit daily. Lest you think you have no sin, consider this: We cannot possibly love God with all our heart, soul, and strength continually nor our neighbor as ourselves. There will always be sins to confess. If left unconfessed, any sin can open a doorway for the devil to destroy.

God is perfect and cannot allow sin in His presence. Whenever sin enters your life or mind, it creates a separation between you and God. Repentance draws you back into His presence. If you want to dwell in the shelter of the Almighty (where there is fullness of joy), confess your sins as soon as possible and often.

What Is Sin?

In general, sin is any action, thought, or feeling that conflicts with God's will and His Law. Below are a few specific examples of sin:

- Pride, arrogance, and domineering attitude
- Bitterness, resentment, and lack of forgiveness
- Dishonoring parents and authority
- Hate, jealousy, racism, and bigotry
- Stealing, killing, and destroying
- Lying, slandering, and gossipping
- Idolizing anything above God
- Lust, adultery, and sexual immorality
- Rebellion against God

Romans 3:23 reveals that all people sin and do not live up to the standards that God has set for us. No one is perfect, but we are called to attempt to achieve that perfection just as Jesus demonstrated for all people. *"He who says he abides in Him ought himself also to walk just as He walked"* (1 John 2:6). True love and commitment to God will manifest in both the desire and the actions to please Him. Jesus says, *"If you love Me, keep My commandments* (John 14:15).

Because we cannot keep the commands perfectly, we must balance out our life with confession of sin. One of the greatest things you can do to obey Christ is to confess daily that you are a sinner in need of His forgiveness. *"If we say that we have no sin, we deceive ourselves, and the truth is not in us. If we confess our sins, He is faithful and just to forgive us our sins and to cleanse us from all unrighteousness. If we say that we have not sinned, we make Him a liar, and His word is not in us"* (1 John 1:8-10).

Forgiveness sets the foundation for all godly relationships. Tomorrow, we are going to start looking at what godly soul ties actually look like. But today, you have some homework to do, and it is going to be a little different than previous days.

HOMEWORK

Pray the following prayer of repentance with a sincere heart before the Lord:

> Good and merciful God, I acknowledge all my sins which I have committed every day of my life, in thought, word, and deed — in body and soul alike.
>
> I am heartily sorry that I have ever offended You, and I sincerely repent.
>
> With tears, I humbly pray to you, O Lord!
>
> According to Your mercy forgive me all my past transgressions and absolve me from them.
>
> I firmly resolve, with the help of Your grace, to amend my way of life and to sin no more, that I may walk in the way of the righteous and offer praise and glory to the name of the Father, Son, and Holy Spirit. Amen!

Pray the prayers on the following pages:

PRAYERS

1. Lord, I acknowledge my faults and failures before you. Let me keep nothing hidden from You.
2. Forgive me for all the times I have not been faithful to Your holy Word.
3. Heavenly Father, I thank you for everything: for salvation and redemption through the blood of Jesus Christ.
4. I confess that I am a sinner, and I acknowledge my sins are ever before you.
5. I repent and renounce all my heart sins, including negative attitudes, false pride, unjust anger, bitter envy, malicious hatred, and lack of forgiveness.
6. I repent and renounce all my sins of action, including immorality, drunkenness, stealing, and blaspheming.
7. I repent and renounce all my sins of neglect, not obeying your Word and commandments.
8. I repent and renounce all the sins of my ancestors, family, nation, community, and church.
9. I repent of all the critical words I have spoken to others.

10. Help me forgive those who have sinned against me in any way.
11. Jesus, I receive You as my Lord and Savior. Help me abide in You, and let Your Word abide in me.
12. Remove from me every bitterness, anger, and resentment.
13. I receive the blood of Jesus as a substitute for my sins.
14. Create in me a clean heart and take not Your Holy Spirit from me.
15. May the blood of Jesus blot out all my transgressions.
16. In the blood of Jesus Christ, I receive mercy, forgiveness, and redemption.
17. Thank You, Jesus, for your mercy and forgiveness toward me.
18. Restore all things Satan has taken, including my health, marriage, children, and destiny.
19. Lord Jesus, I commit to seek first Your Kingdom and righteousness.
20. Use me as You will, in Jesus' name. Amen.

DAY THIRTY

EXPRESSIONS OF GODLY SOUL TIES

*That their hearts may be encouraged,
being knit together in love.*
Colossians 2:2

God the Father, God the Son, and God the Spirit are eternal. Before creating the world, the One God existed in joyful communion with each person of the Trinity. Together, they counseled to create the world and all it contains. Their bond of fellowship set the example for all godly soul ties.

True godly relationships bring a kind of joy that can be found nowhere else. Plus, these relationships are the foundation for a godly society. God desires that His children have the same joys of fellowship that He has in the Godhead. That's why Paul prayed for the saints that their hearts would be "*knit together in love*" (Colossians 2:2). God desires a marvelous expression of godly soul ties. If you are not yet experiencing fullness in godly relationships, don't despair. This book is designed to help you break free from ungodly relationships so you can enjoy the fullness of God's design in your life.

Today, let's explore deeper some of the most significant godly soul ties and discuss some dangers to be aware of in those relationships.

- **Friendships:** God knit the souls of Jonathan and David together in a special friendship. You ought also to have at least one very good friend that you can trust with your life. Jonathan and David were willing to risk their lives for each other. If you want to have a close friend, you must also be a good friend. Jonathan and David both loved God. If your heart is knit to an unbelieving friend, you could set yourself up for danger in the physical and spiritual realms. You should not form soul ties with unbelievers. God says we are not to be yoked together with unbelievers (2 Corinthians 6:14). This doesn't mean all your friends must be Christian. However, you should not tie your soul to non-Christian friends. Rather, you should see them as part of your mission field.

- **Marriage:** Love forms the foundation of all positive and godly soul ties. This occurs most strongly between two people within the bonds of holy matrimony. Marriage unites two souls in a religious ceremony, which is thereafter strengthened through sexual intercourse. *"For this reason a man shall leave his father and mother and be joined to his wife, and the two shall become one flesh"* (Matthew 19:5). We must honor marriage, husbands loving their wives and wives submitting to their husbands.
- **God:** Our strongest soul tie ought to be with God Himself. Deuteronomy 10:20 states, *"You shall fear the Lord your God; you shall serve Him, and to Him you shall hold fast, and take oaths in His name."* According to *Strong's Concordance*, "hold fast" means to adhere or join together. We must be united to Jesus Christ through faith if we desire help in day-to-day struggles, deliverance, and salvation. Our commitment to the Lord and our service to Him creates a very strong soul tie. This allows us to mimic Jesus' declaration: *"I and My Father are One."*
- **Saints:** While we can have a special soul tie with close, believing friends, we also have a unique soul tie with all believers. Ephesians 4:16: *"The whole body, joined and knit together by what every joint supplies, according to the effective working by which every part does its share, causes growth of the body for the edifying of itself in love."* Since all believers are united with Christ, we share a special soul tie. We are called upon to provide assistance to one another in love. Soul ties provide believers the ability to do so. However, we must be careful in our affections with other saints, treating them as fathers, mothers, sisters, and brothers.
- **Animals:** We can have godly affections for animals even though they are not created in the image of God. The prophet Nathan tells the story of a man who had a soul tie with a lamb, loving it like his own child. *"But the poor man had nothing, except one little ewe lamb which he had bought and nourished; and it grew up together with him and with his children. It ate of his own food and drank from his own cup and lay in his bosom; and it was like a daughter to him"* (2 Samuel 12:3). However, our affections for our animals must never be more important than our relationships with humans, who are created in the image of God.

Some godly soul ties exist whether we pursue them or not. For example, if we are in Christ, we are tied to Him and to His body, the church. However, we ought to nourish and cherish these soul ties so they can have full expression.

Other godly soul ties, like friendship, marriage, and children within marriage ought to be sought out. Marriage would be excepted if God has given you the gift of celibacy. Godly soul ties are how godly societies are formed and ordered.

HOMEWORK

Answer the following questions:

1. Why are godly soul ties important to God?

2. What godly soul ties can you thank God for today?

3. Which godly soul ties need strengthening in your life?

4. Can you recognize any dangers in your relationships that might need correcting? Write them down along with one or two solutions.

5. What is one soul tie you can never undo?

6. Pray the prayers on the following page.

PRAYERS

1. Father, thank You for creating godly soul ties.
2. I especially thank You for joining me to the Lord Jesus Christ through faith.
3. Help me foster godly soul ties.
4. Knit my soul together with the friends that You have chosen for me.
5. I desire to experience the fullness of relationships that You have for me.
6. Strengthen the godly bonds in my marriage (or) Help me find a godly spouse.
7. Father, Son, and Holy Spirit make my strongest soul tie be with You.
8. Help me love the saints more, Lord, since we are bound together for eternity.
9. Thank You for animals, Lord. Help me never love them more than humans.
10. Bring me godly relationships so I can be an example to others and build a godly legacy.

DAY THIRTY-ONE

FORMING GODLY SOUL TIES

Be kindly affectionate to one another with brotherly love,
in honor giving preference to one another.
ROMANS 12:2

Have you ever walked into an unfamiliar place and felt completely alone, like an outsider? There were no familiar faces to greet you with a smile, handshake, or hello? Sadly, this even happens in Christian churches. We each desire to connect with others but are often too fearful to be the first one to reach out. Rather than being a victim in these situations, we can be the salve to a lonely soul by taking the initiative to smile and say hello first.

Godly relationships take work, and we can't expect them to pursue us. Rather, we need to be proactive in the process, praying for godly relationships, seeking godly relationships, and strengthening godly relationships. We need godly relationships to help us in our Christian walk. There are no happy "solo" Christians in the kingdom of God.

Foundation of Godly Soul Ties

Biblical love is the foundation of all godly soul ties. Yesterday, we introduced the "Love Test" based on 1 Corinthians 13:4-8. Today, we will explore additional elements of biblical love that should be considered when forming godly relationships.

When seeking out close relationships, be aware of the following principles to see that you are operating according to biblical love. Also, evaluate the friends you choose to "knit" together with to make sure they also understand what true love is.

1. **Law of God:** Jesus identified the two greatest commandments as loving God and loving neighbor. But He didn't stop there. Jesus told His followers to love God and neighbor according to the Law and the Prophets. *"Jesus said to him, 'You shall love the Lord*

your God with all your heart, with all your soul, and with all your mind.' This is the first and great commandment. And the second is like it: 'You shall love your neighbor as yourself.' On these two commandments hang all the Law and the Prophets" (Matthew 22:37-40). We must submit all our relationships to the Lordship of Jesus Christ and to His commandments.

2. **Fruit of the Spirit:** When we become a Christian, we receive the Holy Spirit. As a result, we bear His fruit in our lives. *"But the fruit of the Spirit is love, joy, peace, long-suffering, kindness, goodness, faithfulness, gentleness, self-control* (Galatians 5:22-23). If we are going to be a good friend to someone, we must seek to do by living out the nine-fold fruit of the Spirit (love, joy, peace, patience, kindness, goodness, gentleness, faithfulness, and self-control) in the friendship. Plus, we should seek close friendships that also bear this beautiful and attractive fruit.

3. **Putting Others First:** Remember the example shared earlier? If we are pointing our finger at others for not being friendly, we are thinking of our own needs first. God wants us to consider others as more important than ourselves. The Apostle Paul admonishes us to be like Jesus and *"Let nothing be done through selfish ambition or conceit, but in lowliness of mind let each esteem others better than himself"* (Philippians 2:3). When we seek the needs of others, we open up great opportunities to form strong godly soul ties. However, we ought also see this humility reciprocated in our friendships. If someone else constantly seeks their own way, they are not the kind of person you want to trust with your soul.

4. **Liberty in Christ:** We should never expect a person to conform to our idea of what is right and wrong. Sometimes we have a "pet peeve" or prefer things a specific way. Maybe we like the toilet paper turned in a certain direction or enjoy a particular type of music. We ought not try to force our position upon others but give them the freedom of conscience. *"Stand fast therefore in the liberty by which Christ has made us free, and do not be entangled again with a yoke of bondage"* (Galatians 5:1). If the Bible does not call something sin, we shouldn't call it a sin. We don't want to manipulate or control people to our ways of thinking, nor should we be manipulated or controlled by others.

5. **Self-Sacrifice:** Jesus was the greatest example of love ever. He laid down His life in sacrificial love for us. John 15:13 says, *"Greater love has no one than this, than to lay down one's life for his friends."* True love means we will sacrifice for our friends. Notice though how the passage says that we lay down our lives for our friends. Someone who

asks, forces, or manipulates you into self-sacrifice is not loving at all. Our sacrifices for our friends must come from sincere, heartfelt desires. Plus, we should not try to force our friends to sacrifice for us. Self-sacrifice is voluntary. Otherwise, it is not self-sacrifice.

Tomorrow, we will examine how these five principles might work out in real-life situations with godly soul ties.

HOMEWORK

Answer the following questions:

1. Are you more apt to pursue godly relationships or allow them to pursue you?

2. According to Jesus, what is the foundation of true love?

3. List the five principles of godly relationships mentioned above.

4. In what ways can you improve as a friend?

5. Why is it important to seek godly friendships?

6. Pray the prayers on the following page.

PRAYERS

1. Father, help me be a good friend.
2. Teach me to love according to Your Word.
3. Fill me with the fruit of Your Spirit.
4. Help me to allow my friends the freedom to be who You created them to be.
5. Lord, teach me how to form godly soul ties.
6. So often, Lord, I want to put myself first. Forgive me.
7. Help me listen to others, be patient when wronged, and be kind when I am frustrated.
8. Teach me what it means to sacrifice for others.
9. Bring godly people into my life as examples.
10. Help me choose friends who love according to Your Word, in Jesus' name.

DAY THIRTY-TWO

NAVIGATING GODLY SOUL TIES

*The things which you learned and received and heard and saw
in me, these do, and the God of peace will be with you.*
Philippians 4:9

The best education we can get for developing and growing godly relationships is lived out in the home. Unfortunately, sin has crept even there. Like many others, you may not have had godly relationships or godly soul ties demonstrated in your early years. However, there is still hope because God is our greatest example. And He has given us His Word to guide us. Also, He has given us godly examples in the world, if we will seek them out.

Whether we like it or not, we will mimic those around us. That is why it is vital to surround ourselves with godly men and women worthy of imitating. In this way, we can learn to mimic godly behavior and create thriving soul ties. Jesus was the perfect example of godly living, and the Apostle Paul was another. Paul lived his life in such a way that he could tell others to mimic him. We too should live our life so close to God that we can tell others to mimic us. If you did not have a godly example in your home, God can still raise you up to be a godly example for the next generation. Below are some ways to help you practice godliness in your relationships based on the five points we discussed yesterday.

1. **Marriage:** 1) Our marriages must submit to the Law of God. This means that we must marry in the Lord and keep marriage between one man and one woman. 2) Marriage is the most intimate of all relationships and can be the most difficult to walk in the fruit of the Spirit. According to James 3:2: "*We all stumble in many things. If anyone does not stumble in word, he is a perfect man.*" Marriage is a testing ground for our sanctification. We must work hard to honor God. 3) God has ordained a hierarchical structure in the

family. The man is the head or leader in the home and must love and serve his wife as Christ serves the church. The wife is the husband's helpmeet and is asked to respect him and submit to him as she submits to God. A wife cannot force her husband to love her; he must voluntarily give his love. Likewise, a husband cannot force his wife to submit; she must do so with a willing heart.

2. **Friendships:** 1) A friendship is a mutual fellowship between two people that can form a soul tie. It would be improper for a close fellowship to occur between a man and a woman if they are not pursuing marriage. This is especially true if one of the friends is married to someone else. 2) If a friendship is looking toward marriage, there should be strict boundaries and precautions taken to avoid falling into sexual encounters prior to marriage. 3) Since friendships are mutual, there should be a give-and-take exchange. If one friend is doing all the giving or taking, it is an imbalanced friendship and not a godly soul tie.

3. **Family:** 1) Godly soul ties in families are also subject to biblical restrictions. Parents ought to strive for first-time obedience from their children and seek to shepherd the heart of the child, not merely looking for outward compliance. Plus, fathers are not to exasperate their children by expecting more from them than their age requires. Children are to respect their parents and all those in authority over them. 2) Parents should not meddle in the lives of their adult children, but give godly advice when welcomed. This also applies to family members that do not have direct authority over another family member. 3) Because of the natural inclination to form soul ties among family members, one must be especially careful to guard against predators in the family who might seek to violate or take advantage of a weaker member.

4. **Leadership:** 1) In the church, we must be careful to keep our relationships proper. A male leader should not meet alone with a female that is not his wife. Even if the meeting is well-intended, it can cause an ungodly soul tie to form. 2) Due to the potential to admire someone in a leadership role, it is important not to view them as God. The Apostle Paul highly esteemed the Bereans because they tested to see if the things he taught were found in the Bible. We ought to examine the teachings of our leaders against the Bible. 3) Leaders need accountability. If you are a leader in the church, you should develop godly relationships with other leaders in the church who can hold you accountable.

5. **God:** 1) The godliest soul tie we can form is with God Himself. Since God defines love, we ought to be studying the Bible daily to learn more about His ways. 2) God is perfect

in all His ways and will never seek to manipulate us. However, we can from time to time seek to control God. This is a losing battle. We cannot force God to do anything for us. Be careful not to use words as magic formulas to get God to do your bidding. These kinds of prayers can open you up to demonic soul ties instead of godly ones. 3) Jesus gave His life as the ultimate sacrifice to secure our salvation. We ought also to sacrifice for Him. Some of the sacrifices God loves include, praise and thanksgiving, acts of service, fervent prayer, humble fasting, cheerful giving, and joyful obedience.

While a book could be written on each of the topics above, this chapter provides a great introduction to navigating godly soul ties. God does want all your soul ties to be knitted and formed in Him. Allow God to have mastery over all your friendships and relationships. Only then will you see the fullness of joy that He can bring into your life through godly soul ties. Tomorrow we are going to look at how negative emotions can keep you from establishing godly relationships.

HOMEWORK

Answer the following questions:

1. List any examples where you saw godly soul ties in action growing up.

2. How can you be an example of godly relationships to others?

3. Where do you struggle to maintain godly soul ties? What can you do to improve?

4. Name one relationship you want to work on and write down one step you can take. Take it.

5. How is your relationship with God? What can you do to improve it?

6. Pray the prayers on the following page.

PRAYERS

1. Father, strengthen my godly relationships.
2. Help me put all my family and friends under Your Lordship.
3. Keep all my relationships pure, Lord, so I may be above reproach.
4. Lord, bring me godly relationships that mirror Your love.
5. Help me live my life so close to You that people can look to me as an example of godliness.
6. Father, teach me how to be an example to future generations.
7. Protect me from relationships that will bring me harm.
8. Keep Satan out of all my relationships.
9. Lord, knit my heart to You.
10. May all my prayers be from the heart and not in vain, in Jesus' name. Amen.

DAY THIRTY-THREE

CORDS OF NEGATIVE EMOTIONS

A fool vents all his feelings,
But a wise man holds them back.
PROVERBS 29:11

God created emotions so mankind can "feel" life in a tangible way. Emotions help people "experience" something in a way they can understand. Emotions communicate with our soul, in our soul, and through our soul. Love and joy are two of the highest emotional expressions.

- **Love:** We can feel strong emotions of love toward friends, family, and our spouses. Yet, love is more than just an emotion; it involves action. God demonstrated His love toward us by sending Christ to die for our sins. Sacrificing one's life is the highest expression of love.
- **Joy:** Joy, on the other hand, has no action involved. It is pure emotion. As Christians, we can experience the fullness of joy in Christ Jesus by abiding in Him. Jesus said, *"These things I have spoken to you, that My joy may remain in you, and that your joy may be full"* (John 17:11). What things did He speak? Jesus told the disciples if they wanted to experience the fullness of joy, they needed to stay close to Jesus and obey His commandments (John 15:9-10).

Unfortunately, due to the fall, it is extremely difficult for Christians to experience the fullness of joy that is available.

The Fall's Effect on Emotions

When Adam chose to disobey God in the Garden, He was separated from the presence of God. Before the fall, Adam and Eve experienced the fullness of joy. "*You will show me the path of life; In Your presence is fullness of joy; At Your right hand are pleasures forevermore*" (Psalm 16:11). But their sin separated them from God, and immediately, they began to experience negative emotions, including guilt, fear, and pride.

Negative emotions, when left unchecked and unhindered, hold people in bondage. It is impossible to be in the presence of God when we are given over to the cords of negative emotions. If you want to experience the joy of the Lord, you must cast aside these cords. Let's look at a few negative emotions that can hold you in prison.

Emotions and Soul Ties

Emotions are the glue that creates godly and ungodly soul ties. We should always seek the highest and purest forms of emotions: love and joy. The Bible repeatedly commands us to love one-other and to rejoice always. These two emotions can glue us together with God as we enter His presence and seek His face.

Pure love and joy (not the counterfeits of lust and induced euphoria) ought to mark all our relationships. In heaven, we will experience perfect love and joy. On earth, we are to strive for it by drawing near to God and keeping the commandments.

Negative emotions keep us bound to ungodly soul ties. The purpose of this book is to break free from all ungodly soul ties. To be successful, you will need to become the master of your spirit (emotions).

Seven Negative Emotions

Negative emotions seek to control you. Have you ever experienced a red hot face, pulsing blood, shaking hands, or palpating heart when you've been angry or afraid? Strong emotions release chemicals in your body that can "take over" your soul and make you think, say, or do irrational things. If left unchecked, Satan will take every advantage of your negative emotions to harm you. With the help of the Spirit, you must take the helm of your soul and subdue ungodly reactions from negative emotions. Let's look at a few emotions that you must master.

1. **Anger:** There are times for anger. However, in our anger, we must never sin. Wrongful wrath binds us with destructive cords. The first murder resulted from anger and jealousy.
2. **Fear:** Perhaps you've heard that fear is a liar. A person held bondage to fear will not be free to obey the Lord, experience His joy, or sever ungodly soul ties. It is God alone that we should fear.
3. **Depression:** When our souls are downcast, we are held in bondage to fruitlessness and despair. The result? We might want to sleep all day, not do our work, recoil from people, or ignore our daily activities. We definitely cannot experience the joy of the Lord if we are depressed.
4. **Pride**: Oftentimes, pride stirs us up to harm ourselves. It is a destructive force that can keep us in bondage to bad relationships and destructive behavior. We must snip this cord before it drags us down. God also opposes the proud but gives grace to the humble.
5. **Grief:** While grief is not a sin, it still has the power to hold us captive. It is proper to mourn the loss of a loved one. However, grief must adhere to proper bounds so it does not control you.
6. **Guilt:** Feeling guilty can crush our spirits. And, it is possible to feel guilty even when we've done nothing wrong. We need to give guilt the proper place in our lives. But it should get no more ground than it deserves.
7. **Jealousy:** This negative emotion is akin to covetousness for it wants something that it doesn't own. It could include someone's time, money, belongings, or reputation. Contentedness with godliness is the cure.

Each of these negative emotions also has a positive counterpart, which can make it difficult at times to sort out. Over the next several days, we will examine some of these negative emotions more closely so you can cut the cords.

HOMEWORK

Answer the following questions:

1. Why did God create emotions?

2. Describe the differences between love and joy.

3. Why are negative emotions so dangerous?

4. List the seven negative emotions mentioned in this chapter? Which do you struggle with most?

5. What is the cure for jealousy?

6. Pray the prayers on the following page.

PRAYERS

1. Father, I don't want to be a fool. Help me master my emotions.
2. Lord, I want to experience the fullness of Your joy.
3. Teach me to abide in You and to let Your word abide in me.
4. Bring me into your presence, Lord, so I can experience the fulness of joy.
5. Thank You for demonstrating Your love for me by dying on the cross for me.
6. Cut all the cords of negative emotions in my life, Lord.
7. Help me recognize and forsake ungodly anger, jealousy, guilt, fear, grief, depression, and pride.
8. Protect me from the schemes of the evil one.
9. Forgive me for the times that my emotions have caused me to sin.
10. Teach me to live in continual submission to You, Lord Jesus.

DAY THIRTY-FOUR

CORDS OF ANGER

*Do not hasten in your spirit to be angry,
For anger rests in the bosom of fools.*
ECCLESIASTES 7:9

Anger is a bitter enemy, leading men into grievous sin. According to the Bible, a person who is quick to anger is a fool. Why? Anger can easily lead to murder, mayhem, imprisonment, and death. The first instance of anger in the Bible resulted in murder. Cain and Abel, brothers, each brought a sacrifice to the Lord. God was pleased with Able's sacrifice. Yet, God had no regard for Cain's offering. In response, "*Cain was very angry, and his countenance fell*" (Genesis 4:5).

You could literally see the anger on Cain's face. Anger has the power to manifest in our flesh and contort our faces. God, who could also see into Cain's heart, asked, "*Why are you angry? And why has your countenance fallen? If you do well, will you not be accepted? And if you do not do well, sin lies at the door. And its desire is for you, but you should rule over it*" (Genesis 4:6-7). God invited Cain to bring a pleasing sacrifice to God master his anger before it destroyed him. Cain refused God's counsel and murdered his brother instead. Anger can cause you to sin greatly if not mastered.

Godly Anger

We will further discuss unrighteous anger, but first, we must acknowledge that there is a place for righteous anger. God Himself experiences anger. "*God is a just judge, and God is angry with the wicked every day*" (Psalm 7:11). Since God is without sin, anger itself cannot be a sin. Without sinning, Jesus took a whip and drove out all those who were buying and selling in the temple (Matthew 21:12). Sin, lawlessness, and injustice make God angry, and rightly so.

Because we are made in the likeness of God, we too should be angry over the same things that make God angry. However, we do not have the right to "take vengeance" like Jesus. Vengeance belongs to God alone. Godly anger in us will hate the offense, but love the offender according to the Law of God. This is why the Bible can command us to "'*Be angry, and do not sin': do not let the sun go down on your wrath*" (Ephesians 4:26). In cases of true righteous anger, we must not take vengeance, but leave room for God.

However, godly anger is rare. Most people experience another kind of anger: the anger of man. The Bible warns: "*The wrath [anger] of man does not produce the righteousness of God*" (James 1:20). Rather, it brings about death.

Roots of Ungodly Anger

To break the neck of the beast of anger, we need to identify the root cause. Anger is often merely a symptom of another sin. If we try to fight the anger itself, we may never gain mastery. Let's go back to Genesis to see if there was another sin motivating Cain's anger: "*And in the process of time it came to pass that Cain brought an offering of the fruit of the ground to the LORD. Abel also brought of the firstborn of his flock and of their fat. And the LORD respected Abel and his offering, but He did not respect Cain and his offering. And Cain was very angry, and his countenance fell*" (Genesis 4:3-5).

Do you see it? Cain did not get the same respect as his younger brother. What did Cain want? He wanted God to accept him just like his brother, but without having to do right. Cain was jealous of his brother and guilty of idolatry.

One brother-in-Christ, Steven Sevec, said it like this, "The feeling of anger is a knee-jerk reaction to a negative circumstance that shields the person from dealing with the real emotions they might be feeling in their heart. Anger comes from a sense of entitlement. It stems from unmet expectations. Anger is selfish, petty, and prideful."

Break the Pattern

Now that we understand the basic root of ungodly anger, we can figure out some ways to quash it before it damages your soul or the soul of another. Apply these five steps to break the pattern of anger:

1. **Recognize the Signs:** How does your body react physiologically when you are angry? Does your face turn red? Fists knuckle up? Pulse start pounding? That's your body warning you that you're in danger of sinning.

2. **Identify the Root:** When you experience the signs of anger, look deeper to get to the root cause. Did someone harm you? Are you coveting something that does not belong to you? Do you feel entitled to something that God has not given you?
3. **Confess and Forsake:** Confess both the anger and the root sin that caused the anger. For example, if you are angry because someone was unkind to you, you may need to confess that you are finding your security in how others view you rather than in Christ. Fear of man brings a snare, but he who trusts in the Lord will be exalted. Confess and forsake the sin of fear of man and look to God for your identity.
4. **Memorize Scripture:** Whichever root sin you identified with your anger, find Scripture that speaks to that issue and memorize it. When you find yourself falling again into sin, speak God's Word to your heart by quoting the verse.
5. **Pray Fervently**: Ultimately, God alone can subdue our sinful emotions. Ask Him to reveal the root causes of your anger and to remove them. Also, ask God to revoke Satan's right to use your fallen emotions to harm you.

Bible Verses on Anger

While the verses listed here might not deal with the root of anger, they will provide some additional guidance on how to respond to and think about the negative emotion of anger.

- **Ephesians 4:26:** "'*Be angry, and do not sin*': *do not let the sun go down on your wrath.*"
- **Psalm 37:8:** "*Cease from anger, and forsake wrath; Do not fret—it only causes harm.*"
- **Psalm 103:8:** "*The Lord is merciful and gracious, Slow to anger, and abounding in mercy.*"
- **Proverbs 15:1:** "*A soft answer turns away wrath, But a harsh word stirs up anger.*"
- **Proverbs 16:32:** "*He who is slow to anger is better than the might, And he who rules his spirit than he who takes a city.*"
- **Psalm 19:11:** "*The discretion of a man makes him slow to anger, And his glory is to overlook a transgression.*"
- **Colossians 3:8:** "*But now you yourselves are to put off all these: anger, wrath, malice, blasphemy, filthy language out of your mouth.*"
- **Matthew 5:22:** "*But I say to you that whoever is angry with his brother without a cause shall be in danger of the judgment. And whoever says to his brother, 'Raca!' shall be in danger of the coucil. But whoever says, 'You fool!' shall be in danger of hell fire.*"
- **Proverbs 21:19:** "*Better to dwell in the wilderness, Than with a contentious and angry woman.*"

- **Proverbs 22:24:** *"Make no friendship with an angry man, And will a furious man do not go."*
- **Proverbs 25:23:** *"The north wind brings forth rain, And a backbiting tongue an angry countenance."*
- **Proverbs 29:22:** *"An angry man stirs up strife, And a furious man abounds in transgression."*
- **Galatians 5:22-26:** *"But the fruit of the Spirit is love, joy, peace, longsuffering, kindness, goodness, faithfulness, gentleness, self-control."*

HOMEWORK

Answer the following questions:

1. Why is anger such a dangerous emotion?

2. What is godly anger?

3. How can you discover the root sin of ungodly anger?

4. What are five steps you can take to overcome anger?

5. Which Bible verse mentioned above resonates with your soul? Write it down here and commit to memorizing it.

6. Pray the prayers on the following page.

PRAYERS

1. Father, I don't want to be controlled by anger.
2. Help me recognize the signs in my body that anger is trying to control me.
3. Lord, show me the hidden sins in my life that are at the root of anger so I can forsake them.
4. I reject pride, entitlement, and unmet expectations.
5. I will not give in to selfishness, pettiness, or pride.
6. Cut all the cords of anger in my life, Lord.
7. Destroy Satan's legal ground in my life to use my anger against me.
8. When I sin, help me confess quickly so no bitter root will spring up in my life.
9. When I'm tempted to speak harshly, help me to respond with gentleness.
10. Fill me with the fruit of your Spirit: love, joy, peace, patience, kindness, goodness, faithfulness, gentleness, and self-control.

DAY THIRTY-FIVE

CORDS OF FEAR

*Come, you children, listen to me;
I will teach you the fear of the Lord.*
Proverbs 29:25

The Bible states that God has not given us a spirit of fear. *"For God has not given us a spirit of fear, but of power and of love and of a sound mind"* (2 Timothy 1:7). Yet, elsewhere in the Bible, God commands us *to* fear. *"My son, fear the Lord and the king; Do not associate with those given to change"* (Proverbs 24:21). The question must be asked, "What is fear?"

According to the International Standard Bible Encyclopedia, "Fear is a natural and, in its purpose, beneficent feeling, arising in the presence or anticipation of danger, and moving to its avoidance; it is also awakened in the presence of superiors and of striking manifestations of power, etc., taking the form of awe or reverence." [4] Fear itself has many positive applications for our good. Tomorrow we will dive into the dark side of the emotion of fear. Today, we will evaluate the godly expression of fear because it holds the key to unhinge the cuffs of ungodly fear.

Godly Fear

All emotions have a righteous application in our lives, including fear. God has given us fear to protect us from danger. Let's look at a few examples:

1. **Living Things:** When a vicious dog barks, we should experience enough fear to keep us from petting the dog and being bitten. If a rattlesnake shakes its tail while you are hiking in the desert, you should step in the opposite direction if you don't want to end up with

---

[4] https://www.biblestudytools.com/dictionary/fear/

fang marks in your leg and venom in your body. God has given us a sense of fear to protect us from these creatures.

2. **Civil Rulers:** God has also given fear to help us obey authority. Children ought to fear the rod of reproof from their fathers until they are old enough to know right from wrong. God also commands us to fear civil authorities. *"For he is God's minister to you for good. But if you do evil, be afraid; for he does not bear the sword in vain; for he is God's minister, an avenger to execute wrath on him who practices evil"* (Romans 13:4).

3. **Dangerous Elements:** Good things that God has created, like fire and water, can harm us too. We should all have a righteous fear of fire so that we do not place our hands into a furnace and damage our flesh. We ought to fear drowning enough to teach our children how to swim if they live near water.

These are all rational examples of fear. When we heed this natural and good emotion, we can live life and protect ourselves and others from harm. This kind of fear is given by God for our good. There is an even higher form of fear that protects us from the world, the flesh, and the devil: The fear of God.

The Fear of the Lord

Just as God has given us a bark to help us avoid injuries from a dog attack or a rattle to help us avoid a snake bite, God has given us many warnings in the Bible. For example, God has promised that He will punish evildoers, visit the iniquities of the fathers to the third and fourth generation, and chastise His children for sinning. This knowledge ought to cause us all to have a reverent fear of God's authority, righteousness, and justice. We ought to fear Him as the perfect judge and never trespass on His lovingkindness and mercy.

Plus, the Bible is filled with multiple promises for those who fear Him. Let's look at some of the things promised to those who fear the Lord:

- Secret knowledge (Psalm 25:14)
- Ability to see His covenant (Psalm 25:14)
- God's eye upon you for good (Psalm 33:18)
- The angel of the Lord near you (Psalm 34:7)
- Want of nothing (Psalm 34:9)
- God's favor and mercy (Psalm 103:13,17)
- Wisdom (Psalm 110:10)

- Blessings (Psalm 112:1)
- Knowledge (Proverbs 1:7)
- Long life (Proverbs 10:27)
- Strong confidence (Proverbs 14:26)
- Righteousness (Proverbs 16:6)
- Riches, honor, and life (Proverbs 22:4)
- Safety (Proverbs 29:25)
- Praise (Proverbs 31:30)

What beautiful gifts belong to those who fear the Lord! We serve such a good God. Where else can we go for such amazing benefits? I can think of nowhere but to God alone.

Tremble at His Word

Does fearing God simply mean we are afraid of His judgments and discipline? Absolutely not! It also means we believe in His promises of blessings. *"But without faith it is impossible to please Him, for he who comes to God must believe that He is, and that He is a rewarder of those who diligently seek Him"* (Hebrews 11:6).

Fearing God means that we tremble at His Word. *"For all those things My hand has made, And all those things exist," Says the Lord. 'But on this one will I look: On him who is poor and of a contrite spirit, And who trembles at My word'"* (Isaiah 66:2). When we fear God, we trust in what God says above all else. Fearing God can be synonymous with believing the Bible with our whole hearts. This takes great faith and obedience.

Ungodly fear, on the other hand, is a negative emotion that snares us and holds us captive to ungodly soul ties, harmful relationships, and sin. Fear of God and faith in His Word are the keys to sever all the cords of unrighteous fear. That's what we will look at tomorrow.

Verses to Encourage Godly Fear

Below are some Bible verses to help encourage you in godly fear. Will you tremble at these words and believe them with your heart?

- **Psalm 2:1:** *"Serve the Lord with fear, And rejoice with trembling"*
- **Psalm 22:23:** *"You who fear the Lord, praise Him!"*

- **Proverbs 25:14:** "The secret of the Lord is with those who fear Him, And He will show them His covenant."
- **Matthew 10:28:** "And do not fear those who kill the body but cannot kill the soul. But rather fear Him who is able to destroy both soul and body in hell."
- **Isaiah 66:2:** "'For all those things My hand has made, And all those things exist,' Says the Lord. 'But on this one will I look: On him who is poor and of a contrite spirit, And who trembles at My word.'"
- **Proverbs 18:10:** "The name of the Lord is a strong tower; The righteous run to it and are safe."
- **Psalm 19:9:** "The fear of the Lord is clean, enduring forever; The judgments of the Lord are true and righteous altogether."
- **Psalm 34:11:** "Come, you children, listen to me; I will teach you the fear of the Lord."
- **Proverbs 8:13:** "The fear of the Lord is to hate evil; Pride and arrogance and the evil way And the perverse mouth I hate."
- **Proverbs 14:26:** "In the fear of the Lord there is strong confidence, And His children will have a place of refuge."
- **Proverbs 22:4:** "By humility and the fear of the Lord Are riches honor and life."

HOMEWORK

Answer the following questions:

1. What is fear?

2. Is fear good or bad? Explain.

3. Provide an example of how fear can help protect life and limb.

4. What is the highest form of fear?

5. What are some of the benefits of fearing the Lord? Do you fear Him?

6. Pray the prayers on the following page.

PRAYERS

1. Father, thank You for giving us fear to help preserve life and limb.
2. You have created everything for a purpose, even the rattle on a snake.
3. Teach me to listen to You, Lord, so I may fear You.
4. I receive all the benefits of fearing God.
5. Thank You, Lord, for granting me knowledge, wisdom, riches, honor, blessing, and life.
6. You are a good God, and all your ways are good.
7. Teach me to tremble at Your Word.
8. Help me obey everything that You have commanded.
9. I want to please You, Lord. Grant me faith to believe in Your discipline and Your blessings.
10. Your name is a strong tower, Lord. I will run to it for safety.

DAY THIRTY-SIX

UNGODLY FEAR

There is no fear in love; but perfect love casts out fear, because fear involves torment.

1 John 4:18:

We saw yesterday that godly fear works for our good. It is an emotion that protects us from harm, preserves life, and provides blessings untold in Christ. Ungodly fear, on the other hand, involves torment (1 John 4:18). It is a snare that will trap us and hold us captive until we sever the cords. What is the solution to fear? Love, perfect love.

Perfect Love

It is the love of God that saves us from all the torments of Satan and hell, and God's love never disappoints. "*Now hope does not disappoint, because the love of God has been poured out in our hearts by the Holy Spirit who was given to us*" (Romans 5:5). And what ought to be our response to God's love? We return it back to Him and others by:

- **Loving God:** "*We love Him because He first loved us*" (1 John 4:19).
- **Loving Neighbor:** "*Beloved, let us love one another, for love is of God; and everyone who loves is born of God and knows God*" (1 John 4:7).

Perfect love is a summary of all the teachings of the Bible. "*But whoever keeps His word, truly the love of God is perfected in him. By this we know that we are in Him*" (1 John 2:5). You could even say perfect love is to fear God. "*For this is the love of God, that we keep His commandments. And His commandments are not burdensome*" (1 John 5:3). Jesus testified: "*If you love Me, keep My commandments*" (John 14:15). Solomon concludes the matter: "*Fear God and keep His commandments, For this is man's all*" (Ecclesiastes 12:13).

If you want to escape ungodly fear, *"'Love the Lord your God with all your heart, with all your soul, and with all your mind...and love your neighbor as yourself.' On these two commandments hang all the Law and the Prophets"* (Matthew 22:37). In other words: Fear God!

Now that we know the basic solution to ungodly fear, let's look at some examples of the negative emotion of fear and see how it is built on a bed of lies.

Fear of Man

The Bible says, *"The fear of man brings a snare, But whoever trusts in the Lord shall be safe"* (Proverbs 29:25). The fear of man can express itself in the following ways:

1. **Lying Actions:** When you worry about what others think about you, it can cause you to act in a way that is not true to God or self. For example, if a friend wants to borrow something from you and you really don't want to loan it out, you should say, "No." If you say, "Yes" because you fear that the friend will not like you anymore, you are lying. The Bible says, *"But let your 'Yes' be 'Yes,' and your 'No,' 'No.' For whatever is more than these is from the evil one"* (Matthew 5:37).
2. **Lying Words:** When Abraham was wandering through life, he twice told a "half truth" that put his wife Sarah in grave danger. Why? He was afraid that the people of the land would see how beautiful Sarah was and kill Abraham to take Sarah for themselves. Abraham was not trusting God; he had an ungodly fear of man that caused him to lie in a dangerous way.
3. **Lying Hearts:** Sin likes to hold you in bondage to the fear of man so you will keep sinning in secret. Yet, nothing is hidden from the Lord. He sees all. *"And there is no creature hidden from His sight, but all things are naked and open to the eyes of Him to whom we must give account"* (Hebrews 4:13). If you find yourself sneaking around to sin so others will not see you, then you are in bondage to this ungodly manifestation of fear.
4. **Lying Lips:** Has someone asked you for an opinion, but you were afraid to share your true thoughts? Fear of man can hold you in bondage from speaking the truth in love. Have you heard someone tell a lie about another person without speaking up? Fear has made you complicit in the lie. We are required by God to speak the truth in love (Ephesians 4:15).
5. **Lying Confession:** *"But whoever denies Me before men, him I will also deny before My Father who is in heaven"* (Matthew 10:33). Does fear of man keep you from sharing Christ with your friends and neighbors? *"Therefore whoever confesses Me before men, him I will also confess before My Father who is in heaven"* (Matthew 10:32).

Indeed, fear is a liar. These cords of fear are a trap. Cut and burn them. You cannot fear God if you are trying to please people. *"For do I now persuade men, or God? Or do I seek to please men? For if I still pleased men, I would not be a bondservant of Christ"* (Galatians 1:10). Let the truth set you free.

Irrational Fear

What other things do you fear? Death? Taxes? Spiders? Even the fear of dogs, snakes, governors, rulers, water, fire, or any other created things can be irrational if taken further than God intends. All things must be subject to God's truth. Sadly, Satan can magnify a fear 100X to hold us in bondage to anything if he has legal ground in our life. Ungodly fear itself can give Satan the right to torment you in irrational ways.

Ultimately, all ungodly fear is irrational at the core and stems from a lack of faith. If we believed all the promises in God's word toward those who fear God, there would be no room for false fear in our hearts. Yet, God knows we are but dust. He recognizes our frailties and knows we are weak, fearful people (Psalm 103:14). That's why He has put so many promises in the Bible for us to hold on to — and why He has told us so many times to not be afraid.

Faith Not Fear

If you struggle with the negative emotions associated with irrational fear, the solution is to increase your faith. How do you increase your faith? First, you must dig into God's Word to find out His promises and warnings. Then, you must ask God to implant the Word into your heart through faith. The Bible says, *"So then faith comes by hearing, and hearing by the word of God"* (Romans 10:17).

Also, be honest with God about your present unbelief and ask Him to increase your faith. *"Jesus said to him, 'If you can believe, all things are possible to him who believes.' Immediately the father of the child cried out and said with tears, 'Lord, I believe; help my unbelief!'"* (Mark 9:23-24). Faith is the cure to fear. Do you believe?

Cut the Cords of Fear

Now that you know the cure to fear, let's look at a few steps you can take to help cut the cords that hold you in bondage to sin, self, and Satan.

1. **Seek the Truth:** Since fear is a liar, seek out the truth. Find out everything God says about the topic where you suffer from an ungodly fear.
2. **Identify the Lie:** Now that you know the truth, pinpoint the lie that is causing you to fear something that God doesn't intend.
3. **Confess the Sin:** Ungodly fear will express itself in some form of sin. The fear itself is sin. Plus, you need to confess the lie attached to the sin. Finally, you need to repent of any other sin associated with the fear. For example, if you are afraid (the sin of fear) to share the gospel truth with someone (a form of lying) because they might not want to be your friend (fear of man), you also need to confess the sin of denying Christ before men.
4. **Believe the Truth**: You've discovered the truth, identified the lie, and confessed the sin — now you have to increase your faith so you will believe the truth.
5. **Fear God:** Study all the benefits of fearing God in the Bible and practice the fear of the Lord. If you fear God, ungodly fear will have zero power over you. Remember, perfect love casts out all ungodly fear.

Bible Verses to Ward off Fear

Here are some Bible verses to meditate upon to help you cut the cords of ungodly fear in your life. It is your responsibility to receive them and perceive them. Where you are weak, ask God to help you believe them and achieve them.

- **1 John 4:18:** *"There is no fear in love; but perfect love casts out fear, because fear involves torment. But he who fears has not been made perfect in love."*
- **Proverbs 23:4:** *"Yea, though I walk through the valley of the shadow of death, I will fear no evil; For You are with me; Your rod and Your staff, they comfort me."*
- **Psalm 27:3:** *"Though an army may encamp against me, My heart shall not fear; Though war may rise against me, In this I will be confident."*
- **Psalm 34:4:** *"I sought the Lord, and He heard me, And delivered me from all my fears."*
- **Psalm 56:4:** *"In God (I will praise His word), In God I have put my trust; I will not **fear**. What can flesh do to me?"*
- **Joshua 1:9:** *"Have I not commanded you? Be strong and of good courage; do not be afraid, nor be dismayed, for the Lord your God is with you wherever you go."*
- **Proverbs 29:25:** *"The fear of man brings a snare, But whoever trusts in the Lord shall be safe."*

- **Isaiah 41:10:** *"Fear not, for I am with you; Be not dismayed, for I am your God. I will strengthen you, Yes, I will help you, I will uphold you with my righteous right hand."*
- **Luke 12:7:** *"But the very hairs of your head are all numbered. Do not fear therefore; you are of more value than many sparrows."*
- **Hebrews 13:6:** *"So we may boldly say: 'The Lord is my helper; I will not fear. What can man do to me?'"*

HOMEWORK

Answer the following questions:

1. How does perfect love cast out fear?

2. In what ways can the fear of man be a snare?

3. Explain how fear is a liar?

4. Why is all (ungodly) fear irrational?

5. What is the cure for fear?

6. Pray the prayers on the following page.

PRAYERS

1. Lord, pour Your perfect love into my heart and cast out all my fears.
2. Teach me to love You more and to love my neighbor as myself.
3. Father, I refuse to be snared by the fear of man. I chose to trust in You.
4. Lord, let my "Yes" be "Yes" and my "No" be "No," in Jesus' name.
5. I reject all irrational fear.
6. Jesus, please rebuke all Satan's power in my life due to any sins associated with fear.
7. Grant me the strength and wisdom to always speak the truth in love.
8. Fear of man, you have no power over me, for I fear the Lord.
9. Increase my faith.
10. The Lord is my helper. I will not fear. What can man do to me?

DAY THIRTY-SEVEN

CORDS OF DEPRESSION

Why are you cast down, O my soul? And why are you disquieted within me?
Psalm 43:5

Do you recognize any of these symptoms[5] in your life?

- Feelings of sadness, tearfulness, emptiness, or hopelessness?
- Angry outbursts, irritability or frustration, even over small matters?
- Loss of interest or pleasure in almost all normal activities (like sex, hobbies, or sports)?
- Sleep disturbances, including insomnia or sleeping too much?
- Tiredness and lack of energy, so even small tasks take extra effort?
- Reduced appetite and weight loss or increased food cravings and weight gain?
- Anxiety, agitation, or restlessness?
- Slowed thinking, speaking, or movements?
- Feelings of worthlessness or guilt, fixation on past failures, or self-blame?
- Trouble thinking, concentrating, making decisions, and remembering things?
- Frequent or recurring thoughts of death or suicide or suicide attempts?
- Unexplained physical problems, such as back pain or headaches?

If you are experiencing any of these symptoms, according to the Mayo Clinic, you may have a textbook case of depression. "For many people with depression, symptoms usually are severe enough to cause noticeable problems in day-to-day activities, such as work, school, social activities or relationships with others. Some people may feel generally miserable or unhappy without really knowing why."[6]

---

[5] These symptoms are listed on the Mayo Clinic website here: https://www.mayoclinic.org/diseases-conditions/depression/symptoms-causes/syc-20356007 (Accessed 2/26/21)

[6] https://www.mayoclinic.org/diseases-conditions/depression/symptoms-causes/syc-20356007 (Accessed 2/26/21)

Godly Sorrow

One of the symptoms listed above for depression is "feelings of sadness." Our highest emotion as a Christian is to experience the joy of the Lord. Does that make sorrow a necessarily bad thing? Consider these words from the Apostle Paul in 2 Corinthians 7:9-10: *"Now I rejoice, not that you were made sorry, but that your sorrow led to repentance. For you were made sorry in a godly manner, that you might suffer loss from us in nothing. For godly sorrow produces repentance leading to salvation, not to be regretted; but the sorrow of the world produces death.*

According to the above verse, the Bible teaches that there are two kinds of sorrow:

1. Godly sorrow that produces repentance leading to salvation, not to be regretted; and
2. Worldly sorrow that produces death.

There is a kind of sorrow that is not a negative emotion like depression. Additionally, we may experience sorrow for many righteous reasons: the sin of others; the loss of a loved one; our own sin; a person who is sick unto death; a broken relationship; and more. Never confuse sorrow with depression. Rather, seek to determine if the sorrow is according to the will of God.

Jesus Himself was called a man of sorrows. *"He is despised and rejected by men, A Man of sorrows and acquainted with grief"* (Isaiah 53:3). King David also faced many sorrows that caused him to cry out to the Lord. The Psalms are filled with pleas for relief from sorrow. David wrote, *"Why are you cast down, O my soul? And why are you disquieted within me?"* (Psalm 43:5).

There is a place for sorrow, yet sometimes, our sorrow becomes overwhelming and we get entangled in the cords of depression.

Devastating Depression

A young mother suffering from a broken relationship tells the story of her depression. Her hopelessness was so great, she found herself experiencing the symptoms on the Mayo Clinic's list, including sadness, tearfulness, emptiness, hopelessness, loss of interest in normal activities, lack of energy, feelings of worthlessness, guilt, trouble concentrating, and more.

She would lay on the couch for hours and only do enough to survive. The dishes stacked up, the house got cluttered, and the daughter was left to entertain herself. As the work piled up in the house, the depression only increased to the point of utter hopelessness and despair. Finally, she made a pact with herself and God that no matter HOW she was feeling, every time she found herself on the couch moping, she would get off the couch and clean something. It was not easy to do, but she did it anyway, asking God for help.

Soon, the house was clean. Even though she was still very sorrowful, she was able to function. Eventually, the Lord showed the woman the cause of her depression. She wasn't loving the man who had broken her heart. When she was able to start loving the heartbreaker with actions not just feelings (by being kind, patient, sincere, friendly, caring, etc.), God healed her broken heart. She realized that the man she was coveting after would not even be a good husband or father. Plus, it would have been sinful to get back together with the man because he wasn't a Christian.

Finding Freedom

The mother recounts that though she had recovered greatly from that situation, depression would still chase her down from time to time to bring her back into bondage. Particular types of events would trigger her to become discouraged, including money struggles, work struggles, relationship struggles, or any struggles that caused something to not work out as she wanted, hoped, or dreamed.

As she saw the pattern emerge, she was able to identify the root of her depression. It was always an issue of sin. Ultimately, she was not trusting God with her circumstances. She didn't believe God's promises to provide. There was a time when she even believed that God did not love her. Satan had deceived her and held her captive with cords of ungodly sorrow. Eventually, God completely delivered her.

Steps to Freedom

Not every bout of sorrow leads to depression. However, when sorrow extends the bounds of normal behavior, it should be dealt with swiftly. Here are the steps the mother took to find total freedom from depression.

1. **Pray Continually:** Prayer must accompany every step for healing depression and the symptoms.
2. **Act Anyway:** Usually, emotions control our behavior. However, since we belong to Christ, we have the fruit of the Spirit, including self-control. Make your body submit to Christ regardless of how you feel.
3. **Identify Sin:** Much depression has its roots in unmet expectations. We don't get what we want so our soul gets sad, even mad. In the case of the woman in the story, she wanted

a toxic relationship. Because she couldn't have it, she was unkind and angry toward the father of her child. It started with a sinful relationship. Because she couldn't have it, she was unloving to the man. Finally, she was glued to the couch, neglecting her duties as a mother.

4. **Confess and Forsake:** Once the sin or sins have been identified, they must be confessed and forsaken. The woman had to get back to her duties, forgive the man that had hurt her, and treat him with kindness before she recovered from her depression.
5. **Fear God**: The final step to total healing involves believing the promises of God and learning to love God and your fellow man. This step is a process that must continue until you experience total freedom from depression. It includes memorizing and meditating upon Scripture and asking God to make you believe it with all your heart.
6. **Be Thankful:** There is something about being thankful that will lift your spirit like nothing else. Satan knows this and wants to keep you discontented. No matter how difficult, when you are depressed, start thanking God and see what happens. Use the alphabet as a tool. Find something from A to Z to be thankful for.
7. **Rejoice Always:** If you are joyful, it is impossible to be depressed. Don't rely upon your own joy. Get it from God. *"Do not sorrow, for the joy of the Lord is your strength"* (Nehemiah 8:10).

Roots of Depression

Not all depression is caused by sin. Our souls are made of flesh and spirit that work together cohesively. Below are a few other causes to consider. In all your considering, be sure to take every thought captive to obedience to Christ:

- **Brain injuries:** A hard blow to the head that causes brain damage can rewire the way we think and feel.
- **Sickness and pain:** Strokes, dementia, Alzheimer's Disease, fevers, arthritis, and other illnesses or chronic conditions can lead to feelings of depression also.
- **Illegal drugs:** Not only can drugs provide a doorway for Satanic manipulation of our thoughts and feelings, but they can also cause chemical imbalances in our brains.
- **Prescription medication:** The same is true about pharmaceuticals as illegal drugs. Depression is even listed as a side effect on many prescription drugs.
- **Diet:** The foods you eat affect the way you think and feel. For example, caffeine is stimulant and milk can make you sleepy.

- **Nutritional deficiencies:** Our bodies are designed to thrive on healthy diets. If we are missing a nutrient in our body, it can affect the way we think, feel, and act.
- **Demonic influences:** Satan uses mind control tactics to keep people in bondage to cords of depression.

This list is not comprehensive. However, there is not one illness, sickness, malady, or condition that God cannot heal. If you think your depression stems from demonic forces, engage in spiritual warfare. If you think your depression might be physical, seek God's Word and a trusted physician for healing while engaging in spiritual warfare.

Bible Verses for the Weary Soul

Below are some Bible verses that might be helpful to meditate upon if you are seeking freedom from depression or excessive sorrow.

- **Philippians 4:8-9:** *"Finally, brethren, whatever things are true, whatever things are noble, whatever things are just, whatever things are pure, whatever things are lovely, whatever things are of good report, if there is any virtue and if there is anything praiseworthy—meditate on these things. The things which you learned and received and heard and saw in me, these do, and the God of peace will be with you."*
- **Psalm 34:17:** *"The righteous cry out, and the Lord hears, And delivers them out of all their troubles."*
- **Psalm 3:3:** *"But You, O Lord, are a shield for me, My glory and the One who lifts up my head."*
- **Psalm 32:10:** *"Many sorrows shall be to the wicked; But he who trusts in the Lord, mercy shall surround him."*
- **Psalm 42:11:** *"Why are you cast down, O my soul? And why are you disquieted within me? Hope in God."*
- **1 Peter 5:6-7:** *"Therefore humble yourselves under the mighty hand of God, that He may exalt you in due time, casting all your care upon Him, for He cares for you."*
- **Romans 8:38-39:** *"For I am persuaded that neither death nor life, nor angels nor principalities nor powers, nor things present nor things to come, nor height nor depth, nor any other created thing, shall be able to separate us from the love of God which is in Christ Jesus our Lord."*
- **2 Corinthians 1:3-4:** *"Blessed be the God and Father of our Lord Jesus Christ, the Father of mercies and God of all comfort, who comforts us in all our tribulation, that we may be*

able to comfort those who are in any trouble, with the comfort with which we ourselves are comforted by God."

- **1 Peter 4:12-13:** *"Beloved, do not think it strange concerning the fiery trial which is to try you, as though some strange thing happened to you; but rejoice to the extent that you partake of Christ's sufferings, that when His glory is revealed, you may also be glad with exceeding joy."*
- **Psalm 31:24:** *"Be of good courage, And He shall strengthen your heart, All you who hope in the Lord."*
- **Romans 5:1-5:** *"We also glory in tribulations, knowing that tribulation produces perseverance; and perseverance, character; and character, hope. Now hope does not disappoint, because the love of God has been poured out in our hearts by the Holy Spirit who was given to us."*
- **Romans 8:28:** *"And we know that all things work together for good to those who love God, to those who are the called according to His purpose."*
- **Psalm 32:8:** *"I will instruct you and teach you in the way you should go; I will guide you with My eye."*

HOMEWORK

Answer the following questions:

1. Which items on the list of the Mayo Clinic would the Bible call sin?

2. What is the difference between godly sorrow and worldly sorrow?

3. In the woman's story, what was the root of her depression?

4. What was the first action step the woman took to heal?

5. What steps did she take to find total healing?

6. Pray the prayers on the following page.

PRAYERS

1. Father, help me always examine my sorrow according to Your Word.
2. Thank You for the godly sorrow that leads to salvation.
3. Please reveal any sin in my life that might lead to or contribute to my depression.
4. Lord, I want to experience the fullness of Your joy.
5. Fill me with Your Spirit so I can experience love, joy, peace, patience, kindness, goodness, gentleness, faithfulness, and self-control.
6. Thank You for apples, bananas, chocolate, deliverance, every good and perfect gift, food, grace, etc.
7. Father, heal any brain injuries, illnesses, or nutritional deficiencies that are holding me captive to depression.
8. Forgive me for any substance abuse, Lord. Heal my mind.
9. Revoke all Satanic cords holding me in bondage to depression.
10. Jesus, keep my mind focused on things that are good, true, lovely, excellent, and worthy of praise. Amen.

DAY THIRTY-EIGHT

CORDS OF PRIDE

God resists the proud, But gives grace to the humble.
JAMES 4:6

Beloved, nothing can entangle you more than the sin of pride. It is the fountain of all evil. If you want to break free from all ungodly soul ties and cords of negative emotions, you must tackle pride. In pride, Satan exalted Himself above God. As St. Augustine said, "It was pride that changed angels into devils."

Satan would like nothing more than to see us fall right along with him and his demons. The devil knows that a proud heart cannot fear God, nor can God support a proud person. *"God resists the proud"* (James 4:6). Pride was Satan's poison of choice in the Garden. He tempted Eve to question the authority of God and to be like Him. Pride says, "Has God really said this or that? On the contrary, if you listen to me, you will be like God."

"Sinful pride," says Billy Graham, "is self-centered and boastful, and makes us take credit for everything we are and everything we do. Instead of realizing that we are dependent on God, in our pride we ignore God and believe we can get along without Him."[7] Sinful pride exalts our hearts above God.

Godly Boasting

Not all forms of pride are sinful. If we are going to boast, however, we must boast God's way. Let's look briefly at the kind of boasting and pride that God approves.

1. Boasting in the Lord (Psalm 34:2)
2. Satisfaction in a Job Well Done (Ecclesiastes 3:22)
3. Boasting in Others (2 Corinthians 7:4)

---

[7] https://billygraham.org/answer/can-pride-be-a-good-thing/ (Accessed 2/27/21)

4. Receiving Praise (Proverbs 27:2)
5. Adoring Your Spouse (Song of Solomon 6:9)
6. Honest Appraisal of Gifts (1 Peter 4:10)
7. Boasting in the Truth (2 Corinthians 1:12)

While these are all positive expressions of pride, more often than not, pride expresses itself in oppressive and sinful ways. Let's look at the negative manifestations of pride.

Oppressive Pride

What is the purpose of man? "Man's chief end is to glorify God, and enjoy Him forever."[8] When we live our lives God's way, it brings the fullness of joy. Pride is everything in opposition to God. It seeks to belittle God's glory and take glory to ourselves. The result will be the absence of joy, eternally if we continue in our pride. Pride is a great oppressor of people, holding them in bondage to a lifeless existence away from the presence of God, who opposes the proud, but gives grace to the humble.

Let's look at two characters in the Bible who exhibited great pride against God. One man repents. The other is eaten by worms and sent to hell.

1. **King Nebuchadnezzar:** In a dream interpreted by Daniel, God warned Nebuchadnezzar to repent of his pride. Twelve months later, Nebuchadnezzar looked over his kingdom and said, *"Is not this great Babylon, that I have built for a royal dwelling by my mighty power and for the honor of my majesty?"* (Daniel 4:28). Before he finished speaking, a voice from heaven declared that his kingdom would be taken away and he would eat grass like a beast. That very hour, Nebuchadnezzar *"was driven from men and ate grass like oxen"* (Daniel 4:33) until he acknowledged the God of heaven, recognizing *"those who walk in pride He is able to put down"* (Daniel 4:37). Because Nebuchadnezzar repented, God restored his kingdom. Yet, due to his pride, he ate grass like an ox for seven years.
2. **Herod Agrippa I:** In Acts 12, Luke records some history of Herod Agrippa I, a proud God-hater. He harassed the church of the living God (v. 1), killed James the brother of John (v. 2), arrested Peter and plotted to kill him (vv. 3-4), wrongly executed his own guards (v. 19), and oppressed Tyre and Sidon (v. 20). Finally, he received worship as a god. This was his great undoing. *"So on a set day Herod, arrayed in royal apparel, sat on his throne and*

---

[8] Westminster Confession of Faith Shorter Catechism Q-1/A

gave an oration to them. And the people kept shouting, 'The voice of a god and not of a man!' Then immediately an angel of the Lord struck him, because he did not give glory to God. And he was eaten by worms and died" (Acts 12:21-23).

If you want God to fight for you and not against you, you must cut the cords of pride. *"God resists the proud, But gives grace to the humble"* (James 4:6).

Warnings Against Pride

Ungodly pride is sin (Proverbs 21:4) and it brings all men low, ultimately leading to their destruction (Proverbs 16:16). Anyone who has a proud heart is an abomination to the Lord (Proverbs 16:5). No proud person will escape God's punishment (Proverbs 16:5), and the punishment will extend to an entire home (Proverbs 15:25). Those ensnared in pride do not have an upright soul (Habakuk 2:4), and they lose access to God's power (2 Timothy 3:1-5).

Are you experiencing strife or shame in your home, life, family, or job? *"By pride comes nothing but strife, But with the well-advised is wisdom"* (Proverbs 13:10). Pride wants its own way, humility seeks wisdom from others. When you seek your own way, you will always fail. Ultimately, pride will only bring shame, never the exaltation it seeks. *"When pride comes, then comes shame; But with the humble is wisdom"* (Proverbs 11:2).

17 Indications of a Proud Heart

The sin of pride doesn't always come with great boastings like Nebuchadnezzar or as receiving worship as a god, as King Agrippa I. Rather, sinful pride comes in common expressions of the heart. With all honesty, evaluate these subtle (and not so subtle) signs of pride in your life:

1. Being quick to speak and slow to listen
2. An unwillingness to trust God's Word
3. Exalting science, medicine, or people above the clear teachings of Scripture
4. Interrupting others when they are talking
5. Thinking you know more than others
6. Not being willing to serve in lowly positions
7. Ingratitude for the things you have
8. An unwillingness to seek help or advice from others
9. Dominating conversations

10. More interested in sharing your own ideas than listening to others
11. An attitude of superiority over others
12. Discounting the advice of others without consideration
13. Criticizing others in thoughts or words
14. Needing constant attention and affirmation
15. Having a perfectionist attitude
16. Fear of showing your weaknesses to others
17. Unable to listen to constructive criticism

Do you recognize any of these indicators of a proud heart in your life? Seek the cure A.S.A.P. before God opposes you.

Humility

If you want God to exalt you, then you must humble yourself. Humility is the chief component to fight pride. God gives grace to the humble. He lifts them up. Humility looks to the needs of others. And God commands it. *"Yes, all of you be submissive to one another, and be clothed with humility, for 'God resists the proud, But gives grace to the humble'"* (1 Peter 5:5).

You can experience humility in two ways: either 1) you humble yourself, or 2) God will humble you. When God resists a proud person and brings them low, it hurts. Yet, when we humble ourselves, the only thing that is hurt is our pride. It is in this very state of humility that God will bless us and raise us up. It seems counterintuitive. Yet, it is God's way. Will you resist Him? If so, He will resist you.

Healing A Proud Spirit

Pride is the quintessential sin. You must take every step to correct this monster lest you incur the condemnation of the devil (1 Timothy 3:6). Follow these steps to help cut the cord of ungodly pride.

1. **Humble Yourself:** Humility begins with an action. Every compartment of our soul apart from Christ's grace wants to exalt itself. As God changes your heart, you must take action to humble yourself before God and man. This can be done by fasting and prayer, doing lowly tasks, staying silent under criticism, wearing sackcloth and ashes, blessing those who curse you, and doing the opposite of what your flesh is telling you.

For example, if you want to scream insults at someone for hurting you, speak a kind word to them instead.

2. **Boast in the Lord:** Boast in nothing but the Lord. When you hear your heart or mouth speak proud thoughts, remind yourself of these verses: 1) *"My soul shall make its boast in the Lord; The humble shall hear of it and be glad"* (Psalm 34:2). 2) *"But God forbid that I should boast except in the cross of our Lord Jesus Christ, by who the world has been crucified to me, and I to the world"* (Galatians 6:14).

3. **Give Glory to God:** If we try to take any glory for ourselves, we can expect God to be displeased with us. After many warnings, we might find ourselves eating grass like proud Nebuchadnezzar or eaten by worms like boastful Herod. *"Not unto us, O Lord, not unto us, But to Your name give glory, Because of Your mercy, Because of Your truth"* (Psalm 115:1)

4. **Recognize Nothing Stems from You**: Every breath, skill, talent, resource, friend, wisdom, insight, knowledge, and gift you have comes from God almighty. As He has given, He can take away. Take nothing for granted. When you start to say in your heart, "Look what I can do" or "See how wealthy I am" or "What amazing insights I have" you are subjecting yourself to God's wrath. Instead, say: "See what I can do with Christ's help" or "Thank You, Lord, for giving my wisdom to earn money" or "God has given me wonderful insights." Even our basic needs like daily food come from Him. Never forget to ask Him to provide your daily bread.

5. **Confess Your Pride Daily:** Pride will continually try to take control of your soul. Therefore, you must continually confess your weakness to the Lord and ask Him to help you to humble yourself. Be warned. If you do not humble yourself, God will humble you.

6. **Expect God to Humble You:** If you do not humble yourself, God will humble you. When God humbles a person, it comes at a great cost. Nebuchadnezzar spent seven years eating grass like an animal before he was humbled before the Lord. By God's grace, he repented. Herod, on the other hand, was eaten by worms. This should cause you to fear the Lord and His mighty humbling power — and motivate you to work humility into your own life.

7. **Esteem Others Higher Than Yourself:** Jesus was the ultimate example of humility. He had all the riches in glory and all power and authority, yet He humbled Himself and became a man, laying down His life for His friends. We should follow Christ's example, humble ourselves, and esteem others higher than ourselves. *"Let nothing be done through selfish ambition or conceit, but in lowliness of mind let each esteem others better than himself"* (Philippians 2:3).

Bible Verses to Combat Pride

Study the following verses to remind yourself of the dangers of pride.

- **Proverbs 16:18:** *"Pride goes before destruction, And a haughty spirit before a fall."*
- **2 Chronicles 32:26:** *"Then Hezekiah humbled himself for the pride of his heart, he and the inhabitants of Jerusalem, so that the wrath of the Lord did not come upon them in the days of Hezekiah."*
- **Proverbs 8:13:** *"The fear of the Lord is to hate evil; Pride and arrogance and the evil way And the perverse mouth I hate."*
- **Proverbs 11:2:** *"When pride comes, then comes shame: But with the humble is wisdom."*
- **Proverbs 13:10:** *"By pride comes nothing but strife, But with the well-advised is wisdom."*
- **Proverbs 29:23:** *"A man's pride will bring him low, But the humble in spirit will retain honor."*
- **1 John 2:16:** *"For all that is in the world—the lust of the flesh, the lust of the eyes, and the pride of life—is not of the Father but is of the world."*
- **James 4:6:** *"But He gives more grace. Therefore He says: 'God resists the proud, But gives grace to the humble.'"*
- **Psalm 12:3:** *"May the Lord cut off all flattering lips, And the tongue that speaks proud things."*
- **Psalm 31:23:** *"Oh, love the Lord, all you His saints! For the Lord preserves the faithful, And fully repays the proud person."*
- **Psalm 101:5:** *"Whoever secretly slanders his neighbor, Him I will destroy; The one who has a haughty look and a proud heart, Him I will not endure."*
- **Proverbs 15:25:** *"The Lord will destroy the house of the proud, But He will establish the boundary of the widow."*
- **Proverbs 16:5:** *"Everyone proud in heart is an abomination to the Lord; Though they join forces, none will go unpunished."*
- **Proverbs 21:4:** *"A haughty look, a proud heart, And the plowing of the wicked are sin."*
- **Habakkuk 2:4:** *"Behold the proud, His soul is not upright in him; But the just shall live by his faith."*
- **2 Timothy 3:1-5:** *"But know this, that in the last days perilous times will come: For men will be lovers of themselves, lovers of money, boasters, proud, blasphemers, disobedient to parents, unthankful, unholy, unloving, [b]unforgiving, slanderers, without self-control,*

brutal, despisers of good, traitors, headstrong, haughty, lovers of pleasure rather than lovers of God, having a form of godliness but denying its power. And from such people turn away!"
- **James 4:10:** *"Humble yourselves in the sight of the Lord, and He will life you up."*
- **1 Timothy 3:6:** *"not a novice, lest being puffed us with pride he fall into the same condemnation as the devil."*

HOMEWORK

Answer the following questions:

1. How is pride the fountain of all evil?

2. How did Satan use pride to tempt Eve?

3. What methods may God use to humble pride? Provide examples.

4. Are there any indications in your life that you struggle with pride? List them.

5. What are seven steps to cut the cords of pride in your life?

6. Pray the prayers on the following page.

Prayers

1. Father, I often have a proud heart.
2. I do not want You to oppose me, Lord.
3. Teach me to humble myself in Your sight and the sight of others.
4. Cut the cords of pride in my life so that I can enjoy You forever.
5. Destroy the devil's power in my life due to my sins of pride, boasting, and selfishness.
6. If I boast, let me boast in You, Lord.
7. Forgive me for all the times I have doubted Your Word. Increase my faith, Lord.
8. I revoke all my self-sufficiency and acknowledge that all my gifts, talents, and resources come from God alone.
9. Forgive me for not giving You glory in all things as I ought.
10. Jesus, cleanse me from my pride and selfishness. Remove every wicked way in me. Amen.

DAY THIRTY-NINE

CORDS OF GUILT

*Wash me thoroughly from my iniquity,
and cleanse me from my sin*
PSALM 51:2

Guilt is a beautiful tool in the hands of a loving God to help sinners turn from their sin and be cleansed from all unrighteousness. However, sometimes guilt doesn't work how God intended. We must bring our guilt captive to the Word of God or Satan can use it to hold us in bondage to sin, ungodly soul ties, and toxic relationships. First, we will look at godly manifestations of guilt. Then, we will explore Satan's counterfeit.

Good Guilt

Merriam-Webster rightly defines guilt as "the fact of having committed a breach of conduct especially violating law and involving penalty."[9] Everyone has violated the Law of God and stands guilty before Him. The punishment we all deserve is death. Without this recognition, it is impossible to be saved, for we must each *"Repent, and believe in the gospel"* (Mark 1:15). Without guilt, we would have nothing to repent of.

After we are saved, guilt continues to have a godly role in our lives. Until heaven, we will all continue to sin due to the weaknesses in our flesh that will only be fully solved in glorification. In the meantime, God uses a form of guilt to show us our sins. This guilt is better known as the conviction of the Holy Spirit. When God convicts us of our sin, we must confess our sins to Him. *"If we confess our sins, He is faithful and just to forgive us our sins and to cleanse us from all unrighteousness"* (1 John 1:9).

---

[9] https://www.merriam-webster.com/dictionary/guilt (Accessed 2/27/21)

We can also be "guilty" of covenantal sins that we do not actually commit. These sins can also be confessed, fought against, and forsaken. However, once we have confessed our guilt before God, we no longer stand guilty before Him. The death penalty has already been paid. There is no longer a penalty, though God might discipline us if we stray. Feeling guilty for sins that you have confessed and forsaken is one way Satan can hold you in bondage. We will not take a closer look at ungodly guilt.

Bad Guilt

Any guilt feelings that do not stem from the Holy Spirit's conviction of sin is bad guilt. Plus, there are additional manifestations of satanically inspired guilt. Let's expose the schemes of Satan to counterfeit and confuse guilt.

1. **Guilt Ignored:** If we ignore the conviction of the Holy Spirit for our sin, we can experience a seared conscience. This can lead ultimately to damnation and hell. Satan loves to use this tactic to keep people in bondage to death.
2. **Guilt without True Repentance:** True repentance does more than assuage our guilty conscience, it also bears the fruit of repentance (Matthew 3:8). If we have stolen something, we need to stop stealing and return what was taken (Luke 19:8). Plus, we should work so that we have money to give to the poor (Ephesians 4:28).
3. **Guilt for Past Sins:** Satan would love to keep you feeling guilty for past sins. Why? Because it means you are trusting his lies instead of God's truth that you are forgiven (1 John 1:9). For example, if you have ever shoplifted, you might feel guilty every time you shop. Don't let Satan bring up your sin. Take it to the cross and leave it there.
4. **Guilt for Someone Else's Sin:** People are often held in bondage to the sins of others. Do not feel guilty for someone else's sin. They are responsible before God for their actions, not you. You cannot take upon yourself the guilt of your spouse, children, friends, or pastor. The only exception is if you are participating in the sin or condoning the sin by silence.
5. **Guilt of Shame:** If you have been grossly violated by another person sexually, emotionally, physically, or spiritually, Satan may try to make you feel guilty. You must cast this upon Christ. When you are truly violated, you bear no guilt or shame. If you did participate, confess your part. Then let that cord go for good.

6. **Guilt of Survivorship:** Some people feel guilty when they survive a tragedy that took the life or property of others. If you are alive, do not take that guilt upon yourself. God is in control of life and death. He spared you for a reason. Don't let Satan drag you down because God loved you enough to spare you.
7. **Guilt for Things that Are Not Sin:** Satan loves to make people feel guilty for things that are not sinful. If someone has instructed you that dancing is sinful, take that thought captive to the obedience of Christ. Study the Scriptures and be convinced. However, if you do believe something is sinful and you do it anyway, it is still a sin. Don't hold yourself or anyone captive to guilt that has no place in your life.

In Christ, you are free from all guilt. Positionally, you are declared righteous. When you confess your sins you are forgiven. Feeling guilty after confessing and forsaking sin is a manipulation from the devil to control you. Don't give him that power in your life. Cut the cord!

Healing from a Guilty Conscience

If you struggle with a guilty conscience, follow these steps.

1. **Repent and Believe:** If you have not repented of your sins and believed in the gospel, you *should* have a guilty conscience. If you do not feel guilty, your conscience may be seared. Repent and believe today. Cry out to God for help and forgiveness.
2. **Confess and Forsake:** If you are engaged in ongoing sin, you must confess and forsake them. Are you living with someone out of wedlock? Using drugs? Viewing pornography? Treating people poorly? Examine your heart for any sin that is causing guilt. Confess and forsake it.
3. **Seek Restitution:** If you have taken the first two steps and still struggle with guilty feelings, you might need to make amends in a breached relationship. Are you holding a grudge against someone because they have hurt you? Go talk to that person. Have you wronged someone? Go to them and say you are sorry. Have you stolen? Pay it back. True repentance involves restoring things to the way they should have been before the sin occurred. In as much as you are able, seek restitution.
4. **Believe the Truth:** Are you still feeling guilty? Believe the truth of God's Word that you are forgiven. Accept God's testimony. He does not lie. Satan is the father of lies. He'd love to keep you in bondage to guilty feelings. Trust and obey Christ today: believe the truth. Ask Him to help.

5. **Resist the Devil:** Satan will take every advantage to hold you in bondage to the lies of false guilt. *"Therefore submit to God. Resist the devil and he will flee from you"* (James 4:7). You must stand your ground and put your faith in the truth of God's Word. Speak it back to him if you must. *"There is therefore now no condemnation to those who are in Christ Jesus, who do not walk according to the flesh, but according to the Spirit"* (Romans 8:1).

It is my prayer for you right now that God would deliver you from all false guilt and condemnation as you trust more and more in the power of God for forgiveness.

HOMEWORK

Answer the following questions:

1. Why is guilt good?

2. How does Satan counterfeit godly guilt?

3. What things should you not feel guilty about?

4. Do you struggle with a guilty conscience? Why?

5. What steps do you need to take to rid yourself of ungodly guilt?

6. Pray the prayers on the following page.

PRAYERS

1. Father, I confess I am a sinner.
2. Thank You, Lord, for forgiving me.
3. Please reveal to me any hidden sins so I can confess and forsake them.
4. False feelings of guilt, I reject you, in Jesus' name.
5. I will not feel guilty for sins I have confessed and forsaken.
6. I am not responsible for the sins of others.
7. Father, heal any breaches in relationships that stem from my sin.
8. Help me bear fruit with my repentance so I can have a clear conscience.
9. Destroy any cords of guilt that are built upon the lies of Satan.
10. When false guilt comes upon me, I will submit to You, Lord, and resist the devil, in Jesus' name. Amen.

DAY FORTY

CELEBRATING FREEDOM

*Therefore if the Son makes you free,
you shall be free indeed.*
JOHN 8:36

Beloved, what a journey we have undertaken to achieve freedom from ungodly soul ties and the cords that bind them. Today, we will celebrate by looking at our freedom in Christ. If Jesus sets you free, you are truly free. And what is the tool He uses for your freedom? *"Then Jesus said to those Jews who believed Him, 'If you abide in My word, you are My disciples indeed. And you shall know the truth, and the truth shall make you free'"* (John 8:31-32). True freedom comes from trusting and believing every word that proceeds from the mouth of God.

Many nations and leaders proclaim liberty and freedom. However, true liberty comes from Christ alone. And, by God's grace, when men and nations submit to Christ's Lordship, great blessings abound. He is Lord over all. *"Blessed are all those who put their trust in Him"* (Psalm 2:12). Jesus has the very words of life (John 6:68).

God-Given Liberty

Our liberty is founded upon Christ and His holy Word. We have been using that liberty to break free from yokes and bondage for these past forty days. Let's look deeper at true Christian liberty to relish upon more of what Christ has bought for us.

1. **Life:** Not only is God the giver of physical life, but He is also the author of eternal life. In Christ, we have the freedom to live and breathe. That freedom will last unto eternity.
2. **Joy:** We have the God-given right to pursue the things that bring us joy. Ultimate joy comes from loving God and our neighbor. *"These things I have spoken to you, that My joy may remain in you, and that your joy may be full"* (John 15:11).

3. **Justice:** Jesus came to bring justice and righteousness to the earth. This is part of the freedom He desires. When we apply the principles in the Bible to our life and society, we will see true justice on earth. God cares about the poor and oppressed. *"Who executes justice for the oppressed, Who gives food to the hungry. The Lord gives freedom to the prisoners"* (Psalm 146:7).

4. **Abundant Life:** Jesus wants us to flourish in every way. If someone is seeking to crush your God-given freedoms, you can be sure they are in league with the devil. *"The thief does not come except to steal, and to kill, and to destroy. I have come that they may have life, and that they may have it more abundantly"* (John 10:10).

5. **Deliverance:** Jesus came to destroy the works of the devil (1 John 3:8). That means that God opposes every person, government, or entity that tries to hold people in bondage. God's heart is to *"Deliver the poor and needy; Free them from the hand of the wicked"* (Psalm 82:4).

6. **Freedom:** God wants us to experience total freedom from all sin, oppression, burdens, and yokes. *"Is this not the fast that I have chosen: To loose the bonds of wickedness, To undo the heavy burdens, To let the oppressed go free, And that you break every yoke?"* (Isaiah 58:6). We must use all the means at our disposal to live in His freedom.

7. **Holiness:** Christ did not set us free so that we could sin. That would defeat the whole purpose of dying for us. *"But now having been set free from sin, and having become slaves of God, you have your fruit to holiness, and the end, everlasting life"* (Romans 6:22).

8. **Blessing:** Every spiritual blessing is ours in Christ (Ephesians 1:3). Plus, we have all the promises of Abraham (Galatians 3:14). When we apply God's Word to all of life, we can experience blessings untold. *"But he who looks into the perfect law of liberty and continues in it, and is not a forgetful hearer but a doer of the work, this one will be blessed in what he does"* (James 1:25).

9. **Victory:** In Christ, we have been given authority to trample demons, subdue sin, move mountains, and rule the nations. Christ has commissioned us in His authority. He has all authority in heaven and on earth. Nothing can stop us if we believe. Let's take this world for Christ so that His name will be hallowed in our hearts and our lands. *"The earth is the Lord's, and all its fullness, The world and those who dwell therein"* (Psalm 24:1).

10. **Power:** When we are set free by Christ, we are in-dwelt with the Holy Spirit of power. *"But you shall receive power when the Holy Spirit has come upon you; and you shall be witnesses to Me in Jerusalem, and in all Judea and Samaria, and to the end of the earth"* (Acts 1:8). God wants us to know the exceeding greatness of this power toward us who believe, even His resurrection power (Ephesians 1:19-20).

Indeed, we have victory in Jesus. Let's commit to studying His promises and believing them. *"Eye has not seen, nor ear heard, nor have entered into the heart of man the things which God has prepared for those who love Him"* (1 Corinthians 2:9). Don't be deceived by what you see in the world, in your life, in your finances, or any other thing. Live by faith. *"The just shall live by faith"* (Romans 1:17). Yes. We have much to celebrate indeed. Yet, there are some things that we are not free to do.

Ungodly Freedom

Freedom in Christ has boundaries. We don't want Satan to trick us into celebrating falsely. Let's look at a few things we are not free to do in Christ.

1. **Sin:** We cannot use our freedom in Christ as a license to sin. Satan holds many people captive to lawlessness by tricking them to think they are free from the constraints of the Law. Yes, we are free from the curse of the Law, but we must still keep the commandments. *"For you, brethren, have been called to liberty; only do not use liberty as an opportunity for the flesh, but through love serve one another"* (Galatians 5:13).
2. **Vice:** Nor can we use our freedom as an opportunity to be held captive to vice. *"For this is the will of God, that by doing good you may put to silence the ignorance of foolish men — as free, yet not using liberty as a cloak for vice, but as bondservants of God"* (1 Peter 2:15-16).
3. **Stumbling Block:** Finally, our freedom cannot be used to cause a weaker brother to stumble. For example, if someone believes drinking wine is sinful, you should not entice your brother to drink wine, thereby causing him to stumble. *"So then each of us shall give account of himself to God. Therefore let us not judge one another anymore, but rather resolve this, not to put a stumbling block or a cause to fall in our brother's way"* (Romans 14:12).

Again, these boundaries can be summed up by loving God and loving neighbor. Everything goes back to God's perfect Law, which James calls the Law of Liberty. *"But he who looks into the perfect law of liberty and continues in it, and is not a forgetful hearer but a doer of the work, this one will be blessed in what he does"* (James 1:25). Now that we know the boundaries of our freedom in Christ, let's celebrate some more by looking at the freedoms we gained over the last forty days.

More Freedoms to Celebrate

You have been on a journey now for forty days to break free from ungodly soul ties and create godly ones. Let's celebrate some of the freedoms you have gained by reading this book and applying the principles to your life. You have to freedom to:

1. Identify and destroy ungodly soul ties and relationships
2. Recognize and create godly soul ties and relationships
3. Protect against and sever ungodly generational soul ties
4. Cut off Satanic access to your life and soul
5. Remove the legal ground for Satan to bring harm into your life
6. Know God better
7. Live with blessings and not cursing
8. Break addictions
9. Forgive and be forgiven
10. Heal from soul wounds, soul fragmentation, and demonic introjection
11. Cast away cords of false identity and accept who you are in Christ
12. Break free from deceptive self-talk so you can speak the truth in love
13. Cut the cords of negative emotions, including anger, fear, depression, pride, and guilt
14. Experience the abundant life God has for you
15. Live a life of joy
16. Inherit eternal life

Beloved, you truly are blessed with freedom. God has granted you every spiritual blessing in the heavenly places. If you continue to struggle with any of the above items, go back and reread the chapter or chapters that address these issues. Never stop seeking God. Never stop asking Him to heal you. Never stop asking for total freedom. Never stop celebrating your victory in Christ.

Verses for Freedom

Enjoy your freedom in Christ by memorizing and meditating upon the following verses that talk about freedom, liberty, and justice. All these are ours in Christ Jesus our Lord.

- **Psalm 146:7:** *"Who executes justice for the oppressed, Who gives food to the hungry. The Lord gives freedom to the prisoners."*

- **1 Corinthians 7:22:** *"For he who is called in the Lord while a slave is the Lord's freedman. Likewise he who is called while free is Christ's slave."*
- **2 Corinthians 3:17:** *"Now the Lord is Spirit; and where the Spirit of the Lord is, there is liberty."*
- **Psalm 82:4:** *"Deliver the poor and needy; Free them from the hand of the wicked."*
- **Isaiah 58:6:** *"Is this not the fast that I have chosen: To loose the bonds of wickedness, To undo the heavy burdens, To let the oppressed go free, And that you break every yoke?"*
- **Zechariah 9:11:** *"As for you also, Because of the blood of your covenant, I will set your prisoners free from the waterless pit."*
- **John 8:32:** *"And you shall know the truth, and the truth shall make you free."*
- **John 8:36:** *"Therefore if the Son makes you free, you shall be free indeed."*
- **Romans 6:22:** *"But now having been set free from sin, and having become slaves of God, you have your fruit to holiness, and the end, everlasting life."*
- **Romans 8:2:** *"For the law of the Spirit of life in Christ Jesus has made me free from the law of sin and death."*
- **Galatians 4:31:** *"So then brethren, we are not children of the bondwoman but of the free."*
- **Galatians 5:1:** *"Stand fast therefore in the liberty by which Christ has made us free, and do not be entangled again with a yoke of bondage."*
- **Galatians 5:13:** *"For you, brethren, have been called to liberty; only do not use liberty as an opportunity for the flesh, but through love serve one another."*
- **James 1:25:** *"But he who looks into the perfect law of liberty and continues in it, and is not a forgetful hearer but a doer of the work, this one will be blessed in what he does."*
- **James 2:12:** *"So speak and so do as those who will be judged by the law of liberty."*
- **1 Peter 2:15-16:** *"For this is the will of God, that by doing good you may put to silence the ignorance of foolish men—as free, yet not using liberty as a cloak for vice, but as bondservants of God."*

HOMEWORK

Answer the following questions:

1. How can we have true liberty?

2. What are ten liberties that we have in Christ?

3. What does liberty in Christ NOT mean?

4. Reflect on your 40-day journey to freedom from soul ties. What growth have you seen in your life?

5. What areas in your life still need healing? Make a plan to achieve total freedom in Christ.

6. Pray the prayers on the following page.

PRAYERS

1. Thank You, Jesus, for setting me free.
2. Give me Your Spirit, Lord, in greater measure, for where Your Spirit is there is liberty
3. I want to experience abundant life, joy, justice, deliverance, and freedom to its fullest, Lord. Help me.
4. Make me holy, Lord. Shower me with every blessing in Christ.
5. Grant me victory and power, Lord.
6. Show me the great and wonderful things You have planned for those who love You.
7. Let me never use my freedom as a license to sin, an opportunity for vice, or to cause a brother to stumble.
8. Thank You for this journey, Lord. Continue healing me.
9. Continue to break the power of sin and Satan in my life until I can enjoy the fullness of Your joy.
10. I love You, Lord. Help me love You and my neighbor as I ought, in Jesus' name. Amen.

ABOUT THE AUTHOR

J. E. Charles

Pastor J. E. Charles is the Founder and Senior Pastor of the Upper Room Fire Prayer Ministries and the Dunamis Christian Community Center, a non-denominational, Spirit-led, multi-cultural Christian organization in California. There, he has preached the gospel of Jesus Christ as Senior Pastor since 2013 and was ordained officially on May 21, 2015, in Houston, Texas.

One driving purpose of Pastor Charles' ministry is passionate prayer to assist with the deliverance and healing of people who are physically, emotionally, and spiritually sick. Some call him "a warrior to the core" when it comes to battling demonic and ungodly powers. His dedication to evangelizing, teaching, and preaching focuses on the Kingdom of Christ and an aggressive type of spiritual warfare based on the motto: "*The violent taketh it by force.*" Pastor Charles has been involved in the deliverance ministry for almost 30 years.

Coming from a culture of overt demonic activity, Pastor J. E. Charles battled against generational spiritual forces that had established firm control over multiple people in his circles of influence. He believes that open confrontation with the enemy works best against the forces of darkness. Part of Charles' mission is to teach and guide Christians to take bold and aggressive measures against demonic threats. In turn, he guides believers to discover god-honoring spiritual, financial, emotional, and physical breakthroughs in their lives, their families, and their communities.

Pastor Charles holds leadership positions at the Intercessory Prayer and Freedom Ministries at the Well Christian Community Church, a ministry with the Redeemed Christian Church of God (RCCG), and at the Mountain of Fire and Miracles Ministries in California. People who know him well bestowed upon the nickname, "Mr. Prayer."

Through these leadership roles, Charles offers insights into deliverance, gives wisdom as one who proclaims the mysteries of God, and assists people to understand how to apply God's revelation to their personal life. His goal is to teach believers how to align their life and spirit with God's Word and power.

Pastor J. E. Charles has a heart and vision to see the glory of God manifest in the lives of others. This vision allows him to serve the Dunamis Christian Community in the full power of the Spirit. The deliverance and healing teams in the church reach out to transform those who are trapped by ungodly forces and held captive by their sin. The end goal of his ministry and the Dunamis Christian Community is to lead people to accept Christ, welcome Him into their hearts, and to live in obedience to His revealed will.

Pastor J. E. Charles also delivers public speaking engagements, coaches' people spiritually, and has authored several books. He also offers Christian-oriented business management consultancy services.

The Bible verses that drive Pastor J.E. Charles to a ministry of deliverance include:

- Isaiah 5:13 (KJV): *"Therefore my people are gone into captivity, because they have no knowledge: and their honorable men are famished, and their multitude dried up with thirst."*
- Psalm 7:9: *"Oh, let the wickedness of the wicked come to an end, but establish the just."*
- Obadiah 1:17: *"But on Mount Zion there shall be deliverance, and there shall be holiness; and the house of Jacob shall possess their possessions."*